T0328411

Cambridge Elements ☰

Elements in Public and Nonprofit Administration
edited by
Andrew Whitford
University of Georgia
Robert Christensen
Brigham Young University

PUBLIC SERVICE MOTIVATION AND PUBLIC OPINION

Examining Antecedents and Attitudes

Jaclyn S. Piatak
University of North Carolina at Charlotte

Stephen B. Holt
University at Albany, State University of New York

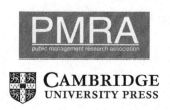

CAMBRIDGE
UNIVERSITY PRESS

University Printing House, Cambridge CB2 8BS, United Kingdom

One Liberty Plaza, 20th Floor, New York, NY 10006, USA

477 Williamstown Road, Port Melbourne, VIC 3207, Australia

314–321, 3rd Floor, Plot 3, Splendor Forum, Jasola District Centre, New Delhi – 110025, India

79 Anson Road, #06–04/06, Singapore 079906

Cambridge University Press is part of the University of Cambridge.

It furthers the University's mission by disseminating knowledge in the pursuit of education, learning, and research at the highest international levels of excellence.

www.cambridge.org
Information on this title: www.cambridge.org/9781108964005
DOI: 10.1017/9781108966672

© Jaclyn S. Piatak and Stephen B. Holt 2021

First published 2021

A catalogue record for this publication is available from the British Library.

ISBN 978-1-108-96400-5 Paperback
ISSN 2515-4303 (online)
ISSN 2515-429X (print)

Additional resources for this publication at www.cambridge.org/piatak

Public Service Motivation and Public Opinion

Examining Antecedents and Attitudes

Elements in Public and Nonprofit Administration

DOI: 10.1017/9781108966672
First published online: February 2021

Jaclyn S. Piatak
University of North Carolina at Charlotte

Stephen B. Holt
University at Albany, State University of New York

Author for correspondence: Jaclyn S. Piatak, jpiatak@uncc.edu

Abstract: Practitioners, policy makers, and scholars across fields and disciplines seek to understand factors that shape public opinion and public service values, especially in today's polarized context. Yet we know little about how the two relate. Research on public service motivation (PSM), a drive to help others grounded in public institutions, has grown to examine career decisions and behaviors within and outside the workplace, but does the influence of PSM extend to individual values? Using data from the Cooperative Congressional Election Study surrounding the 2016 US presidential election, we first examine the antecedents of PSM: How do individual characteristics as well as socioeconomic and sociocultural factors influence levels of PSM? Second, we describe the role PSM plays in shaping public opinion on policy preferences, budget priorities, and political behaviors. Findings have implications for understanding both who has PSM as well as how PSM shapes public preferences, attitudes, and behaviors.

Keywords: PSM antecedents, public opinion, public service motivation, policy preferences, political participation

ISBNs: 9781108964005 (PB), 9781108966672 (OC)
ISSNs: 2515-4303 (online), 2515-429X (print)

Contents

1 Introduction

We see many calls to serve. From volunteer appeals drawing upon inspirational quotes from Dr. Martin Luther King ("Life's most persistent and urgent question is, what are you doing for others?") to poets like Ralph Waldo Emerson ("It is one of the most beautiful compensations of life, that no man can sincerely try to help another without helping himself."). The role of service and cooperation in the United States can be traced back to Alexis de Tocqueville's 1831 visit to America (de Tocqueville, 1831), as he describes:

> As soon as several of the inhabitants of the United States have taken up an opinion or a feeling which they wish to promote in the world, they look out for mutual assistance; and as soon as they have found each other out, they combine. From that moment they are no longer isolated men, but a power seen from afar, whose actions serve for an example and whose language is listened to. (109)

As a result, we often see calls to service in US presidential inauguration speeches, from President John Kennedy's (1961) often quoted "And so, my fellow Americans: ask not what your country can do for you – ask what you can do for your country" to President George H. W. Bush (1989):

> I have spoken of a Thousand Points of Light, of all the community organizations that are spread like stars throughout the Nation, doing good. We will work hand in hand, encouraging, sometimes leading, sometimes being led, rewarding ... The old ideas are new again because they're not old, they are timeless: duty, sacrifice, commitment, and a patriotism that finds its expression in taking part and pitching in.

During his term, President George H. W. Bush signed the National and Community Service Act of 1990, creating a new federal government agency to oversee national volunteering programs, now called the Corporation for National and Community Service. In highlighting the passage of the latest reauthorization, the Edward M. Kennedy Serve America Act of 2009, Michelle Obama emphasized, "Service is a part of who we are as Americans," and House Speaker Nancy Pelosi stated, "In these great times of great challenge, America needs more people like all of you- rolling up your sleeves and pitching in to turn challenges in your communities into opportunities to serve" (Corporation for National and Community Service, 2009). Service is at the heart of our American democracy.

However, social capital has been on the decline (e.g., Putnam, 2000) and the United States is facing increasing polarization from the labor market to politics to societal values. The government has become the bearer of risk as the United States faced three major shocks in recent decades: the terrorist attacks of September 11, 2001, the Great Recession of 2009, and the 2020 pandemic (Roberts, 2020). As we write this, our country faces not only the global

COVID-19 pandemic but also social unrest following the killing of George Floyd during an arrest, bringing attention to both police conduct and racism in our society. These events have shined a bright light on and exacerbated inequities and divisions across the nation (e.g., Gaynor & Wilson, 2020; Wright II & Merritt, 2020). Scholars emphasize the need to overcome political divisions in favor of collaboration and argue: "To fully understand the crisis and response, research will need to incorporate constructs that capture ideology or values of elected leaders and their constituents" (Hall et al., 2020, p. 591).

Political ideology explains a proportion of the public's views across a range of issues (Lauderdale, Hanretty, & Vivyan, 2018), but a significant proportion remains. In light of growing political polarization, Banda and Kirkland (2018) illustrate that higher party polarization in state legislatures reduces citizen trust in their state policy makers. Increasing polarization has led to not only a lack of trust in government among the public and a lack of consensus building among lawmakers, but also polarization of the American public by political party affiliation (Hetherington & Rudolph, 2015). Assessments of candidate traits are increasingly polarized (Hetherington, Long, & Rudolph, 2016), and both Democrats and Republicans increasingly dislike members of the opposing party (Iyengar, Sood, & Lelkes, 2012). With party identification driving clear divides, scholars are searching for a means to explain and reduce intergroup conflict. Yet greater empathy corresponds to higher polarization and greater partisan bias (Simas, Clifford, & Kirkland, 2020). With Americans increasingly divided by political party, could public service motivation (PSM) provide a common ground of concern for others rooted in public institutions?

Across fields and disciplines, scholars strive to understand what drives individuals, from managers wanting to understand employee motivation to politicians and policy makers wanting to understand public opinion. In public management, research on PSM has gained significant traction. Perry and Wise (1990) first defined PSM as the "predisposition to respond to motives grounded primarily or uniquely in public institutions" (368). While conceptually PSM would extend beyond the workplace, and empirically, research finds high-PSM individuals enact more prosocial behaviors both within and beyond the workplace, we know little about how PSM might shape an individual's attitudes and policy preferences. In addition, research on the antecedents of PSM are largely mixed (see Pandey & Stazyk, 2008; Ritz, Brewer, & Neumann, 2016). Therefore, we ask:

- Who has PSM? More specifically, what individual characteristics, socioeconomic factors, and sociocultural factors shape PSM?
- Can and does PSM drive public opinion? More specifically, how does PSM influence US public policy preferences and budget priorities?

As we discuss throughout this Element, particularly in the remainder of this section, the theoretical foundation of PSM lies in an individual's intrinsic valuation of broader public ideals, such as protecting the rights of others, belief in a civic duty to serve the public interest, or the importance of responsibly serving one's community and nation. In short, the concept and the instruments developed to measure PSM to date focus on a predisposition toward compromise, service, and the rights of others. Thus PSM might reflect a broad set of shared values important for identifying common ground across partisan identity and policy preferences that may reflect these broader values. Unfortunately, to date, little empirical attention has been given to the linkages between PSM, political identity, and policy preferences.

Our purpose throughout this Element is to offer a first look at these relationships, using a national sample in the United States, to fill this gap and motivate additional attention from the research community on how latent values and motivations relate to political and policy preferences. We view this work as useful not only for informing the theoretical refinement of the PSM concept but also for understanding what values underly public opinion that may in turn shape policy making, either directly through the decision making of elected officials and administrators alike or indirectly through the role of public opinion in the policy making process. For instance, framing policies linked to PSM in appeals to public values or the broader public interest may be an effective route to building support in policy making and implementation. Additionally, PSM may guide administrative decision making or administrators may find appeals to public values or to the broader public interest useful in aiding the successful implementation of some programs but not others.

In the remainder of this section, we define PSM and highlight the value of the concept. We then provide an overview of the current literature on both the antecedents and consequences of PSM.

In the following sections of this Element, we present our findings and their implications for both research and practice. We describe our data, a national sample of adults surrounding the 2016 US presidential election, variables, and methods in Section 2. We present our findings on how individual demographics and characteristics as well as socioeconomic and sociocultural factors shape PSM in Section 3. We discuss our findings on how PSM relates to policy preferences and budget priorities in Section 4. In light of the role PSM plays in prosocial behaviors outside the workplace, we also examine whether the influence of PSM extends to political engagement and political behaviors in Section 4. We then place our findings in the context of prior work, discuss the implications of our results, and raise avenues for future work in Section 5. We conclude with a summary of our key findings and contributions in Section 6.

1.1 Defining PSM

The groundwork for PSM began with studies examining public/private differences (e.g., Allison, 1980; Boyne, 2002; Perry & Rainey, 1988; Rainey, 2014; Rainey, Backoff, & Levine, 1976; Rainey & Bozeman, 2000) and the values of public service, such as fairness and benevolence (Frederickson, 1997), as well as representativeness (Mosher, 1968). At their core, these studies recognized that public management is different. Public administration is a separate field of study due to the need to connect political science with the management of government and nonprofits, as well as to connect businesses and organizations with social purposes. But scholars like us continue to wonder: Does something unique draw people to public service?

While research highlights important differences across job sectors (e.g., Piatak, 2015, 2017, 2019; Holt, 2018, 2020), PSM scholarship demonstrates that the public service ethos to help others is boundaryless. Individual career decisions are based on numerous factors (for a review of sector motivations, see Piatak, forthcoming). Just because a person leaves a government agency or nonprofit organization may not mean they lost their motivation to serve others, nor does working for a for-profit company mean someone has no desire to serve the public interest. Research on sector switching illustrates those in for-profit organizations move to the public sector in pursuit of intrinsic rewards (Bozeman & Ponomariov, 2009; Georgellis, Iossa, & Tabvuma, 2011), and government employees often stay to serve society (Hansen, 2014). Interestingly, government and nonprofit employees who volunteer are also less likely to move out of public service (AbouAssi, McGinnis Johnson & Holt, 2019), perhaps illustrating the need for PSM driven individuals to serve others regardless of within or outside of the workplace. With the growth of corporate social responsibility, social enterprise, and paid volunteer service hours, people may find ways to fulfill their PSM in opportunities that were unimaginable decades ago.

A unique feature of PSM is the multi-motive nature of the concept. Perry and Wise (1990) envisioned PSM encompassing rational (self-interest), normative (values), and affective (emotions) motives. People are complex and most decisions, actions, and views are not based on a singular motive. We see this as one of the benefits of PSM over related concepts in other disciplines (for a review, see Koehler & Rainey, 2008; for examples, see Piatak & Holt, 2020a, 2020b). Based on the original conceptualization of PSM (Perry & Wise, 1990), there are several rational reasons to serve the public, such as participating in the policy process, personally identifying with the program, or advocating for a special interest. Whether working in government, volunteering, running for office, or making everyday decisions as a citizen such as what cause to support, these rational reasons may play a role. From the norm-based perspective, Perry and Wise (1990) suggest PSM includes a sense of loyalty and duty to the government, a desire to enhance social equity, and a desire to serve the public interest. Here, too, one can see these values as core to many Americans, regardless of their career goals, as these are some of the values at the foundation of our democracy. People are not only driven by reason and values but are also emotional beings. As such, PSM includes the affective motives of conviction of social importance and care for others, or what Perry and Wise (1990) dub willingness to sacrifice for others.

In light of the multi-motive aspect of PSM, Perry (1996) later developed a PSM survey and put forth four dimensions of PSM: commitment to the public interest, attraction to policy making, compassion, and self-sacrifice. Scholars have called for an examination of the dimensions (e.g., Wright & Grant, 2010), used the dimensions in examining how PSM corresponds to individual behavior (e.g., Clerkin et al., 2009; Piatak, 2016a), and called for specific dimensions to be transported to other disciplines (Perry & Vandenabeele, 2015). PSM measurement has received a great deal of attention, including creating alternate scales (e.g., Coursey & Pandey, 2007; Kim et al., 2013; Perry, 1996; Vandenabeele, 2008a). However, many raise issues with the multidimensional approach and highlight the benefits of the global scale (e.g., Piatak & Holt, 2020a; Vandenabeele, Ritz, & Neumann, 2018; Wright, Christensen, & Pandey, 2013). In pursuit of parsimony and coherence (Gerring, 1999), as well as to reap the benefits of a multi-motive construct, we focus on the overall concept (and measure) of PSM rather than a dimensional approach.

These multi-motives can be used to explain many decisions, behaviors, and views. Of course, people driven by PSM may pursue careers oriented toward serving the public, but PSM may have a much broader application. For example, an individual may consciously decide to be more supportive of Black-owned businesses to support the social justice movement. Rational: This individual may personally identify as Black or with the Black Lives Matter movement or this individual may want to be an ally or anti-racist. Normative: this individual may care deeply about social equity or the public interest. Affective: This individual has a genuine conviction to anti-racism or cares about others and our country and so is willing to sacrifice support for one business over another. In a simple choice, of perhaps which restaurant to order takeout from, people inherently evoke multiple types of motives. If PSM captures the public-oriented motivation behind everyday decisions, behaviors, and preferences, then its reach extends well beyond public management.

While PSM originated from examinations of what draws people to public service (Rainey, 1982), PSM extends beyond the public sector. As Perry and

Hondeghem (2008) argue, PSM may "transcend the public sector, that is, characterize motivations in other areas of society that involve the pursuit of the public good" (3). Definitions of PSM illustrate the broad reach of the concept. PSM has been defined as follows:

- "the motivation people have to serve others and contribute to the welfare of society at large" (Brewer, Ritz, & Vandenabeele, 2012, p. 1)
- "motivational force that induces individuals to perform meaningful public service" (Brewer & Selden, 1998, p. 417)
- "denotes the idea of commitment to the public service, pursuit of the public interest, and the desire to perform work that is worthwhile to society" (Scott & Pandey, 2005, 156)
- "a mix of motives that drives an individual to engage in an act that benefits society" (Taylor, 2007, p. 934)
- "a cluster of motives, values, and attitudes on serving the public interest" (Taylor, 2008, p. 67)
- "the belief, values and attitudes that go beyond self-interest and organizational interest, that concern the interest of a larger political entity and that motivate individuals to act accordingly whenever appropriate" (Vandenabeele, 2007, p. 547)

Due to the reach of PSM, scholars call for PSM research to establish conceptual boundaries (e.g., Ritz, Brewer, & Neumann, 2016; Bozeman & Su, 2015; Vandenabeele, Brewer, & Ritz, 2014). Many scholars include other concepts, such as altruism, within definitions of PSM. For example, Perry and Hondeghem (2008) define PSM as "individual motives that are largely, but not exclusively, altruistic and are grounded in public institutions" (6), and Rainey and Steinbauer define PSM as "a general altruistic motivation to serve the interests of a community of people, a state, a nation, or humankind" (23). Piatak and Holt (2020a, 2020b) find that while altruism and PSM have some overlap, they are distinct concepts and PSM is a more consistent predictor of prosocial behaviors. We define PSM as the drive to help others, based in public institutions.

1.2 Why Motivation Matters

Motivation plays a central role in human behavior. For organizations, personal motivation shapes administration behavior (Simon, 2013). How to motivate employees is one of the central questions facing public management (Behn, 1995). As such, PSM research has grown dramatically to examine the motivation and behaviors of public employees. Indeed, Vandenabeele, Brewer, and Ritz (2014) suggest PSM as a means to motivate public employees, promote prosocial behavior, and connect public institutions to their core values.

PSM research tends to focus on government employment. This is largely due to origins (Perry & Wise, 1990; Rainey, 1982) that grew out of studies on public and private differences (e.g., Boyne, 2002; Perry & Rainey, 1988; Rainey, 2014; Rainey, Backoff, & Levine, 1976; Rainey & Bozeman, 2000) and public values (Frederickson, 1997; Mosher, 1968), as well as the data available. In a review essay, Ritz, Brewer, and Neumann (2016) find about three quarters of empirical work on PSM uses public sector data. Little work has examined PSM across job sectors. Instead, job sectors are often used as a proxy for PSM. However, the influence of PSM extends beyond government and even beyond the workplace.

Employees are whole people. What motivates an individual to join public service or exert extra effort at work may influence individual behavior and attitudes outside of the workplace. While the debate over whether PSM is a stable trait (e.g., Holt, 2018; Witteloostuijn, Esteve, & Boyne, 2017; Wright, Hassan, & Christensen, 2017), malleable state (e.g., Vandenabeele, 2011; Ward, 2014), or both continues, we follow Perry and Wise's (1990) conception that PSM is, at least in part, a *predisposition*. Surely, "the relation between motives and action is not usually simple; it is mediated by a whole chain of events and surrounding conditions" (Simon, 2013, p. 157). PSM can be enhanced and inhibited by the context of the world and interactions with others, but some people seem to care more about public service than others. We see PSM as a trait that may increase or decrease based on an individual's surroundings and interactions.

Understanding PSM, who tends to have higher levels of PSM, and how this shapes public policy preferences and priorities has several important implications. First, the influence of PSM may extend beyond behaviors to policy views. Public opinion shapes policy making and, in turn, policy outcomes. As such, public opinion plays a predominant role in policy-making theories, from helping to open policy windows (Kingdon, 1995) to explaining periods of policy instability and change (Baumgartner & Jones, 2010). In this sense, PSM may be a factor in understanding public support for certain policies and policy changes in the United States.

Second, PSM may influence the priorities, decisions, and actions of public employees. Since high-PSM individuals may be drawn to public service positions (e.g., Clerkin & Coggburn, 2012; Holt, 2018; Piatak, 2016a; Stritch & Christensen, 2016; Vandenabeele, 2008b; Wright, Hassan, & Christensen, 2017), understanding how PSM shapes policy preferences and priorities provides insights into the priorities of government employees, nonprofit employees, and policy makers, to the extent individuals sort into such positions.

Lastly, PSM may be a useful concept for other fields and disciplines, including political science. As an interdisciplinary field, public administration tends to borrow and build upon theories from other fields and disciplines. PSM is one of the few concepts to originate in public administration and public management (Meier, 2015; Piatak & Holt, 2020a). With increasing applicability (Perry & Vandenabeele, 2015), perhaps PSM is a useful concept to understand not only motivation for behaviors to advance public service, but also attitudes about public service and how to serve the broader public.

1.3 Antecedents of PSM

Along with questions of why people are motivated come questions of who is motivated by PSM. Considering the positive outcomes of PSM, scholars have examined the antecedents. However, since PSM originated out of studies on motivation to join public service (e.g., Rainey, 1982), research tends to focus on how organizations and management can inhibit or enhance PSM (for a review, see Harari et al., 2017). While the question of whether PSM is an inherent trait, dynamic state, or both remains, we follow the perspective that PSM is a predisposition. As such, we focus on the influence of *individual* characteristics, socioeconomic, and sociocultural factors in shaping PSM. Outside of the workplace setting, what factors shape an individual's PSM?

Despite the research attention on the determinants of PSM (for reviews, see Pandey & Stazyk, 2008; Parola et al., 2019), research is largely mixed, particularly for our understanding of how demographic characteristics relate to PSM. For example, reviews on age and gender illustrate a mix of conflicting findings and null results (Ritz, Brewer, & Neumann, 2016). Studies are largely limited by the data available. Most work on the antecedents of PSM use samples of government employees (e.g., Bright, 2005; Camilleri, 2007; Vandenabeele, 2011), those in public service (e.g., Charbonneau & Van Ryzin, 2017), or volunteers (e.g., Perry et al., 2008), which biases the sample toward people already drawn to service.

Since PSM extends beyond the workplace, who exhibits higher levels? Using a national sample of US adults, we examine the influence of individual characteristics, socioeconomic factors, and sociocultural factors in Section 3. But first, we review what we know about who has higher levels of PSM.

1.3.1 Individual Characteristics

Sociodemographic characteristics are primarily control variables in examinations of PSM (Pandey & Stazyk, 2008), but there has been some work on the antecedents of PSM and these largely begin with demographics (e.g., Bright, 2005; Perry, 1997; Vandenabeele, 2011). Research tends to find higher levels of PSM with age and among women, but there are important nuances, discussed as follows.

Age

Research on the relationship between age and PSM has drawn upon psychological theories of development (e.g., Pandey & Stazyk, 2008). In particular, Erickson's (1963) generativity helps explain why the desire to make the world a better place for future generations and to have an enduring impact increases with age. As an individual gets older, the desire to have a positive influence on society and guide younger generations increases. A meta-analysis of thirty studies finds support for PSM increasing with age, but also finds this may vary by country context (Parola et al., 2019). Some find PSM declines with age, such as in the context of state civil servants in Flanders (Vandenabeele, 2011) and among Maltese public officers (Camilleri & Van Der Heijden, 2007), while Perry (1997) finds PSM increases with age in the United States.

Gender

Women tend to be more other-oriented. Research consistently finds women are more likely to volunteer than men (e.g., Musick & Wilson, 2008; Piatak, 2016b; Piatak, Dietz & McKeever, 2019), as women have a greater sense of obligation to help others (Musick & Wilson, 2008). Riccucci (2018) suggests biology, psychology, and socialization shape women's predisposition to a more nurturing nature, certain value system, and socialization into gender roles that align with PSM. Despite nuances across dimensions (Camilleri, 2007; DeHart-Davis, Marlow, & Pandey, 2006), women tend to have higher levels of PSM than men (Bright, 2005; Parola et al., 2019; Vandenabeele, 2011).

The individual attributes examined depend largely on government surveys available (like the Merit System Protection Board Survey; e.g., Naff & Crum, 1999) or those gathered (like the National Administrative Studies Project; e.g., DeHart-Davis, Marlow, & Pandey, 2006). Since surveys of government employees tend to require a partnership or at least approval of a government entity, the data gathered is sometimes limited. For example, detailed information on race and ethnicity is collected in the Federal Employee Viewpoint Survey but not shared publicly (e.g., Nelson & Piatak, 2019). While some studies examined racially underrepresented groups broadly, no significant results were found in relation to PSM (Bright, 2005; Charbonneau & Van Ryzin, 2017). This may be due to differences across racial groups that disappear when grouped into a binary white, non-white indicator.

We build upon the growing work on individual characteristics to examine not only age and gender, but also the influence of race, ethnicity, sexuality, and transgender in shaping an individual's PSM.

1.3.2 Socioeconomic Factors

Socioeconomic factors may also play a role in shaping PSM. However, only education has received any significant attention.

Education

Education is the most consistent predictor of PSM (Pandey & Stazyk, 2008). Indeed, PSM research finds those with higher levels of education have higher levels of PSM (Bright, 2005; Camilleri, 2007; Perry, 1997; Vandenabeele, 2011). This may be due to the socialization effect of education (e.g., Elchardus & Spruyt, 2009; Stubager, 2008). For example, MPA students have higher levels of PSM compared to MBA students (Van der Wal & Oosterbaan, 2013). Similarly, government professionals with a background in public administration or political science view their role as policy making more than those who studied other fields (Piatak, Douglas, & Raudla, 2020). While these are specific to degree programs, the act of pursuing each level of education may expand an individual's world view and social network.

We know far less about the social factors of marital status and having children, as well as the economic factors of employment and income. Using a dimensional approach to PSM, Camilleri (2007) finds those married with children at home have a higher commitment to the public interest and compassion, but we know little of the independent influences. Few have examined employment and income since many of the studies are based on government or public service employees. However, Perry (1997) found income had a negative influence on PSM. Perhaps those with higher incomes are more business-oriented and less service-oriented. Due to largely employee samples and work-focused surveys, we know little about how socioeconomic factors, aside from education, shape PSM.

We examine not only the role of education but also the potential influence of family and employment status, such as marital status, presence of children, disability, employment status, and income, on PSM.

1.3.3 Sociocultural Factors

People are shaped by their beliefs, values, and socialization. As a result, socialization has received a great deal of attention in the PSM antecedents literature. However, this work largely focuses on one's upbringing (e.g., Charbonneau & Van Ryzin, 2017; Perry et al., 2008) and organizational influences (for a meta-analysis, see Harari et al., 2017). How do current sociocultural factors outside of the workplace influence PSM?

We focus on two factors that are often studied in relation to public opinion (e.g., Zaller, 1992) but less frequently in PSM research: the role of politics and religion.

Political Ideology

Politics play a key role in the US, especially with the growing political polarization. People are shaped by their values, including political ideology and political party. In turn, political parties may have a socialization influence on an individual's level of PSM, particularly for those who play an active role. As such, scholars have examined the influence of both political parties and political ideologies on PSM. Using a dimensional approach, Perry (1997) found a more conservative ideology corresponds to a greater attraction to policy making but lower levels of self-sacrifice. In examining the influence of family background, Charbonneau and Van Ryzin (2017) find individuals raised by a conservative family have lower levels of PSM. Turning from political ideology to party, Vandenabelee (2011) finds Christian Democrats reported higher levels of PSM, while those in the Extreme Right reported lower levels of PSM. Research tends to find those with a more conservative ideology have lower levels of PSM. Perhaps this reflects conservatives being more family-focused rather than other-oriented.

Religiosity

As a religiously diverse country, religion plays a large role in both uniting and dividing the US public (Putnam & Campbell, 2012). Since religion provides a basis for individual beliefs, values, and socialization, scholars have examined religion as an antecedent to PSM. A majority of this work finds religion has a positive influence, from a scale of religious activities (Perry et al., 2008) to the religiosity of an individual's family (Charbonneau & Van Ryzin, 2017) to an individual's own religiosity (Witteloostuijn, Esteve, & Boyne, 2017). However, while Perry (1997) found "closeness to god" to have a positive influence on PSM, more active church involvement was associated with lower levels of PSM. Measures of religiosity range from personal beliefs to religious practices (e.g., Pearce, Hayward, & Pearlman, 2017). While Perry et al. (2008) find religious activity to be one of the strongest predictors in their study of award-winning volunteers with interviews supporting the role of spirituality, there are many measures of religion and religiosity that need disentangling.

To advance our understanding of the role of politics, we examine both the influence of political ideology and political party on PSM. To better understand the role of religion, we examine both the influence of religiosity, measured by the level of church attendance, and the type of religion on PSM.

1.4 Consequences of PSM

PSM has become a predominant concept in public and nonprofit management (for reviews, see Perry & Hondeghem, 2008; Perry & Vandenabeele, 2015; Ritz,

Brewer, & Neumann, 2016; Vandenabeele, Brewer, & Ritz, 2014). Research on PSM tends to focus on one of several areas: career choice, employee behaviors, and prosocial behaviors outside of the workplace. One challenge of advancing research on the behavioral outcomes of PSM is the use of job sector as a proxy for PSM. To provide some clarity, we specify whether studies examine PSM or job sector and highlight those using direct measures of PSM.

Considering the many benefits of PSM, both within and outside of the workplace, we suggest PSM may be a useful construct in predicting individual preferences and attitudes beyond the workplace. Could PSM help predict public policy preferences?

1.4.1 Career Choice

Since PSM grew out of early studies on sector differences (e.g., Perry & Rainey, 1988; Rainey, 1982; Rainey, Backoff, & Levine, 1976), research has focused on the relationship between PSM and job sector. Explaining why people pursue public service careers was part of the original conceptualization, as Perry and Wise (1990) asserted: "the greater an individual's public service motivation, the more likely the individual will seek membership in a public organization" (370). Drawing upon Schneider's (1987) attraction-selection-attrition framework, people will be attracted to public service in order to satisfy their PSM. Research generally supports that people with higher levels of PSM pursue and choose public service, broadly defined to include government and nonprofit sector work.

PSM is higher in the public sector and those with higher levels of PSM exhibit public sector preferences. The prevalence of PSM in the public sector can be seen in comparisons of PSM-related values across job sectors (e.g., Brewer, 2003; Houston, 2000; Lewis & Frank, 2002; Steijn, 2008). More directly, scholars find PSM corresponds to a preference to work in the public sector (Clerkin & Coggburn, 2012; Piatak, 2016a; Sanabria-Pulido, 2018; Stritch & Christensen, 2016; Vandenabeele, 2008b). While findings vary across dimensions (e.g., Ballart & Rico, 2018; Clerkin & Coggburn, 2012; Pedersen, 2013; Piatak, 2016a; Rose, 2013; Vandenabeele, 2008b), the global measure is a consistent predictor of public sector preferences (Korac, Saliterer, & Weigand, 2019; Piatak, 2016a). As a result, reviews conclude PSM corresponds to public sector work (Asseburg & Homberg, 2020; Ritz, Brewer, & Neumann, 2016), but more recently also acknowledge that organizational context plays a role (Asseburg & Homberg, 2020).

People may be attracted to a certain type of work rather than a specific job sector. For example, in an examination of law students, Christensen and Wright

(2011) find those with higher levels of PSM are more likely to accept a job that emphasizes service regardless of the job sector. Similarly, some find the ability to make a difference may be more important than working in the public sector (e.g., Chetkovich, 2003; Tschirhart et al., 2008). Research finds PSM may be more related to the nature of public sector work, rather than the sector itself (Andersen, Pallesen, & Pendersen, 2011; Kjeldson & Jacobsen, 2013). For example, using a panel of Dutch social workers across sectors and a dimensional approach to PSM, Kjeldson (2014) illustrates the role of PSM in predicting work tasks. The relationship between PSM, sector, and work task is complex.

However, recent work illustrates the role of PSM in shaping job sector preferences. In a longitudinal study, Holt (2018) finds PSM-related values predict public sector employment. This supports the idea that individuals with high levels of PSM may select into public service. Similarly, using panel data, Wright, Hassan, and Christensen (2017) show that PSM during law school predicts one's job sector several years after graduation.

While the attraction versus socialization debate continues, research illustrates the relationship between PSM and the job sector is more complex than originally thought (e.g., Kjeldson, 2014). Recent job advertisement experiments illustrate the complexity of job preferences and the role of PSM (Asseburg et al., 2020). Attraction and selection into a given position or career entail a variety of factors, including organizational preferences, occupational preferences, and task preferences, in addition to job sector preferences. While many factors contribute to job sector differences (for a review, see Piatak, forthcoming), PSM plays a significant role.

If PSM is part of the puzzle in explaining complex individual decisions like employment choices, perhaps PSM can explain broader public preferences and the priorities of government and nonprofit policy makers and decision makers.

1.4.2 Employee Behaviors

Research highlights the influence of PSM on employee behaviors within the workplace. As such, PSM has significant implications for human resource management (for reviews, see Christensen, Paarlberg, & Perry, 2017; Piatak, Sowa, Jacobson, & McGinnis Johnson, 2020). Scholars have found many positive influences of PSM on employee behavior and work attitudes. Drawing upon the fit literature (for a review, see Kristof-Brown et al., 2005), high-PSM individuals are expected to not only pursue, but also be more satisfied and excel in positions and organizations and with groups and supervisors that align with their PSM.

PSM corresponds to job satisfaction. Many individual studies (e.g., Andersen & Kjeldsen, 2013; Steijn, 2008; Taylor, 2007, 2008) and reviews (Homberg,

McCarthy, & Tabvuma, 2015) find a positive relationship between PSM and job satisfaction. Since much of this works focuses on government employees, it is perhaps unsurprising that government employees with higher levels of PSM will be more satisfied in public service. Indeed, Kjeldsen and Hansen (2018) find PSM has a positive impact on job satisfaction for those in the public sector compared with those in the for-profit sector. However, some highlight the role of person-organization or person-job fit (Bright, 2008; van Loon, Vandenabeele, & Leisink, 2017; Wright & Pandey, 2008), as well as goal clarity and congruence (Jensen, Andersen, & Jacobsen, 2019; Wright & Pandey, 2011), that may matter more than PSM. As such, PSM has both direct and indirect effects on job satisfaction through fit (Kim, 2012) and perceived job impact (Taylor, 2014). High-PSM individuals in public service tend to be more satisfied with their work, but fit, value congruence, and organizational context play a role.

PSM-driven employees tend to go above and beyond at work. Many find those with higher levels of PSM exhibit organizational citizenship behavior (OCB) and extra-role behaviors (e.g., Boyd et al. 2018; Campbell & Im, 2016; Gould-Williams, Mostafa, & Bottomley, 2015; Ingrams, 2020; Pandey, Wright, & Moynihan, 2008; Piatak & Holt, 2020b; Ritz et al., 2014; Shim & Faerman, 2017; Van Loon, Vandenabeele, and Leisink, 2017). This holds across job sectors (Ingrams, 2020), and PSM is found to be a stronger predictor than related concepts like altruism (Piatak & Holt, 2020b). However, recent work cautions about the "dark side" of PSM and meaningful work, such as presenteeism (Gross, Thaler, & Witner, 2019; Jensen, Andersen, & Holten, 2017; Oelberger, 2019), without proper management support. Perhaps there is a cost to caring too much or of managers or coworkers taking advantage of PSM-driven employees who are willing to go the extra mile.

Related to the extra effort of PSM-driven employees, research finds a link between PSM and performance (e.g., Andersen, 2009; Andersen, Heinesen, & Pedersen, 2014; Vandenabeele, 2009). For example, in a field experiment, Bellé (2013) finds baseline PSM strengthens the influence of the interventions on the performance of nurses in a public hospital. While there are many ways to think about and measure performance, one that should play a central role in the public sector is ethics. PSM-related measures are found to reduce unethical judgments (Ripoll & Breaugh, 2019), and PSM is associated with greater ethical obligations for less professionalized employees (Stazyk & Davis, 2015). In addition to PSM, management can play a role in enhancing whistleblowing behavior (Davis, Stazyk, & Klingeman, 2020; Ripoll, 2019a; Wright, Hassan, & Park, 2016). According to Ripoll (2019b), motivation and ethics are both embedded into an individual's identity, where PSM can be understood as a public service moral identity.

How might this PSM-driven obligation to further the public interest influence preferences, behaviors, and decisions outside of the workplace? PSM has been critiqued for a lack of research on the role of PSM in decision-making (O'Leary, 2019), but scholars have begun to examine the role of PSM in decision-making and policy preferences. Using a survey experiment administered to students and three dimensions of PSM, Moynihan (2013) finds PSM unrelated to budget recommendations. However, prior work suggests PSM may influence policy making and implementation. For example, Huang and Feeney (2016) find high PSM local government managers are more likely to use citizen participation in decision-making. In addition, Song et al. (2017) find high PSM bureaucrats prefer more direct policy instruments. Perhaps such policy preferences extend beyond the workplace.

To advance our understanding of how PSM may influence decisions, we examine how PSM shapes public policy preferences and budget priorities.

1.4.3 Prosocial Behaviors

The prosocial behaviors of high-PSM individuals extend beyond the workplace. Using job sector as a proxy for PSM, scholars find those in public service are more likely to volunteer, particularly in the nonprofit sector and at the local level (Holt, 2020; Piatak, 2015). Using more direct measures of PSM, scholars find PSM positively corresponds to volunteering, both for certain dimensions (Clerkin et al., 2009) and global measures of PSM (Christensen et al., 2015; Clerkin & Fotheringham, 2017; Piatak, 2016a; Piatak & Holt, 2020; Walton et al., 2017). Testing the boundaries of PSM, Piatak and Holt (2020b) find PSM to be a better predictor of prosocial behaviors than altruism, particularly in more formal contexts like volunteering with an organization.

PSM has drawn much attention for its positive influence on behaviors both within and outside of the workplace, from high-PSM individuals helping and putting in extra effort at work to volunteering with formal organizations and in the community. Given the role of elected officials and politics in shaping our public institutions, does the influence of PSM extend to political engagement and behaviors?

Scholars note that political positions have received little attention (Ritz, Brewer, & Neumann, 2016). However, research examines how PSM corresponds to the behaviors of local government councilmembers. Ritz (2015) finds high PSM Swiss councilmembers, in terms of the attraction to policy making and commitment to the public interest dimensions, are more likely to seek re-election and spend more time on party activities. While PSM was found unrelated to re-election intention among Danish councilmembers, PSM has a positive influence on self-reported political influence (Pendersen, Andersen, & Thomsen, 2020). PSM seems to play a role in the motivation and effort put forth by councilmembers, but what about broader political engagement?

We now turn to examine how PSM corresponds to political engagement from deciding to run for office to attending local public meetings to working on political campaigns.

2 Methods

To examine who has PSM and whether it plays a role in shaping public opinion, we draw upon data from the University of North Carolina at Charlotte (UNCC) survey module of the 2016 Cooperative Congressional Elections Study (CCES). Studies of PSM are largely limited to student samples or government-employee samples organized by individual scholars or projects (e.g., the National Administrative Studies Project) or federal government surveys (e.g., the Merit Principles Survey). While this is appropriate when examining important public management questions like what motivates employees or how motivation influences employee behavior, the data limit the reach of PSM research to government, or public service more broadly, and often the workplace. While scholars have examined the benefits of PSM outside of the workplace (see Section 1.4.3, "Prosocial Behaviors"), few examine broader populations (for exceptions, see Holt & Piatak, 2020a; 2020b). The CCES not only gives us the opportunity to examine a broader sample of US adults but also asks a wider array of questions due to both the original survey module and the nature of the survey.

2.1 Data

The CCES is a national stratified sample survey of more than fifty thousand individuals administered online by YouGov. The survey is organized by a team of scholars and has a cooperative structure that pools resources across research teams. The CCES was first launched in 2005 with the goal of overcoming issues of scale, content, funding, and coordination, as well as a lack of consistency in federal government surveys (Ansolabehere & Rivers, 2013). The CCES produces results that mirror voting turnout (Ansolabehere & Schaffner, 2014), election results and findings from the American National Elections Study (Ansolabehere & Rivers, 2013), and phone surveys (Ansolabehere & Hersh, 2012). The study is composed of common content, identical across all research teams, and team content, the unique data for each research team module. Further details about the CCES, including access to common content, may be found online (https://cces.gov.harvard.edu/) and details about the matched-random-sampling methodology for 2016 CCES can be found in Ansolabehere and Schaffner (2017).

The UNCC team module includes the global measure of PSM that makes it possible for us to examine the broader antecedents of PSM as well as the relationship between PSM and public opinion. The survey questions were asked of a subsample of one thousand respondents.

2.2 Public Service Motivation (PSM)

Reliable and reproducible measurement presents a long-standing difficulty for studying motivating values, such as altruism, prosocial motivation, and PSM. Much of the early scholarship on PSM focused on developing and testing survey scales that could produce reliable measures of the construct in order to better relay how PSM operates in the real world (see, for instance, Kim et al. 2013; Perry, 1996;Wright et al., 2013). As with most measures of latent factors, researchers face a trade-off between precision in the measure, through the use of sixteen-item (Kim et al., 2013) or twenty-four-item (Perry, 1996) survey scales that seek to include measures of all dimensions of PSM, and the cost of data collection when using scales with a large number of survey items.

We adopt a global measure of PSM, the five-items originally included on the Merit System Protection Board Survey (the MSPB5 scale; e.g., Alonso & Lewis, 2001; Naff & Crum, 1999), to measure respondents' relative levels of PSM. The global scale contains five items that ask respondents to determine the degree to which they agree or disagree that a particular statement applies to themselves using a five-point Likert scale. The statements target different dimensions of PSM, such as self-sacrifice (e.g., "I am prepared to make sacrifices for the good of society"), compassion (e.g., "I am often reminded by daily events about how dependent we are on one another"), and public interest (e.g., "Meaningful public service is very important to me"). The measure has the advantage of being validated in prior work (e.g., Wright et al., 2013), as it has been included on government surveys at the federal (e.g., Merit System Protection Board Survey) and state (e.g., National Administrative Studies Project) levels and in numerous individual studies. Some argue the field may be better served to focus on the global measure (e.g., Vandenabeele, Ritz, & Neumann, 2018) and highlight the benefits of the global measure (e.g., Piatak & Holt, 2020b).

Results often vary across dimensions and studies but are consistent when the global measure is used. For example, public sector career preferences vary across dimensions and studies (Ballart & Rico, 2018; Clerkin & Coggburn, 2012; Pedersen, 2013; Piatak, 2016a; Rose, 2013; Vandenabeele, 2008b), but the global measure consistently corresponds to a preference for

Table 1 PSM measures

1. Meaningful public service is very important to me.
2. I am often reminded by daily events about how dependent we are on one another.
3. Making a difference in society means more to me than personal achievements.
4. I am prepared to make sacrifices for the good of society.
5. I am not afraid to go to bat for the rights of others even if it means I will be ridiculed.

public sector employment (Korac, Saliterer, & Weigand, 2019; Piatak, 2016a). Similarly, some find certain PSM dimensions correspond to volunteering (Clerkin et al., 2009; Piatak, 2016a), but greater consistency is found for the global measure (Christensen et al., 2015; Clerkin & Fotheringham, 2017; Piatak, 2016a; Piatak & Holt, 2020b; Walton et al., 2017). Therefore, in the interest of conceptual clarity, in terms of parsimony and coherence (Gerring, 1999), we employ the commonly used five-item global measure of PSM.

We use a standardized index of the principal components of the five-item global measure (see Table 1 for the five items derived from Perry, 1996; for a discussion of the Merit Principles Survey items, see Alonso & Lewis, 2001; Naff & Crum, 1999; for a discussion of the global measure, see Piatak, 2016a; Wright, Christensen & Pandey, 2013). The index has an interitem correlation of 0.35 and Cronbach's alpha of 0.77, providing strong statistical evidence that the measure reliably captures the latent construct of interest, PSM.

2.3 Dependent Variables

We first examine the factors that correspond to higher levels of PSM in Section 3, where PSM is our dependent variable. We then turn to examine how PSM corresponds to public policy preferences, budget priorities, and political behaviors in Section 4. Here, PSM becomes our independent variable of interest, and our dependent variables are the policy preferences, attitudes, and political behaviors.

2.3.1 Who Has PSM?

Our analysis begins by descriptively examining average differences in levels of PSM across groups of people. Since a variety of experiences may shape the motivating values (like PSM) that people hold, comparing PSM across groups of people who differ in their educational background, economic profile, religious views, political ideologies, and demographics in a national sample can provide insights into the social experiences associated with varying levels of PSM. We investigate group differences in PSM using descriptive regressions that adjust for other characteristics in our comparisons. For readers less interested in the technical details, we present the findings of our analysis in Section 3.

2.3.2 PSM and Public Opinion

A core question animating our study involves the potential link between individuals' level of PSM and their policy preferences, budget priorities, and political behaviors. We investigate this relationship using a mix of preelection survey items regarding policy views and post-election survey evaluation of government services and political behaviors. Our findings are presented in Section 4.

Policy Preferences

Given increasing polarization in the United States, PSM may provide insights into public preferences beyond political ideology and political party. To address this question, we examine a range of policy issues across levels of government intervention. Past work on PSM, suggests high PSM street-level bureaucrats prefer direct policy instruments (Song et al., 2017), but how might PSM shape broader public policy preferences?

We measure policy preferences using two items from the preelection survey. The first asks respondents whether they support or oppose specific policies regarding gun control, abortion, gay marriage, immigration, environmental regulations, and crime. For each policy, we create a binary indicator for whether a respondent supports a given policy proposal.

- For gun control, respondents were asked whether they support or oppose the following policies: background checks for all sales, including at gun shows and over the Internet; prohibiting state and local governments from publishing the names and addresses of all gun owners; banning assault rifles; and making it easier for people to obtain concealed-carry permits.
- For abortion policies, respondents were asked if they support or oppose always allowing a woman to obtain an abortion as a matter of choice; permitting abortion only in case of rape, incest, or when the woman's life is in danger; prohibiting all abortions after the twentieth week of pregnancy; allowing employers to decline coverage of abortions in insurance plans; prohibiting the expenditure of funds authorized or appropriated by federal law for any abortion procedures; and making abortion illegal in all circumstances.

- Despite the US Supreme Court overturning the Defense of Marriage Act and legalizing same-sex marriage in 2013, policies continue to infringe on the rights of LGBTQ individuals, including recent religious exemptions. Respondents were asked whether they favor or oppose gay marriage.
- To assess environmental policy preferences, respondents were asked whether they support or oppose the following policies: giving the Environmental Protection Agency the power to regulate carbon dioxide emissions; raising the required fuel efficiency for the average automobile from 25 mpg to 35 mpg; requiring a minimum amount of renewable fuels (wind, solar, and hydroelectric) in the generation of electricity, even if electricity prices increase somewhat; and strengthening the enforcement of the Clean Air Act and Clean Water Act, even if it costs US jobs.
- For immigration, respondents were asked whether they support the following policies: granting legal status to all illegal immigrants who have held jobs and paid taxes for at least three years and have not been convicted of any felony crimes; increasing the number of border patrols on the US-Mexican border; granting legal status to people who were brought to the United States illegally as children but who have graduated from a US high school; fining US businesses that hire illegal immigrants; admitting no refugees from Syria; increasing the number of visas for overseas workers to work in the United States; identifying and deporting illegal immigrants; and banning Muslims from immigrating to the United States.
- To examine public views on criminal justice policies, respondents were asked whether they support or oppose eliminating mandatory minimum sentences for nonviolent drug offenders; requiring police officers to wear body cameras that record all of their activities while on duty; increasing the number of police on the street by 10 percent, even if it means fewer funds for other public services; and increasing prison sentences for felons who have already committed two or more serious or violent crimes.

The second measure of policy preferences asks respondents whether they would vote for or against a series of legislation and appointments under consideration in Congress if they were, themselves, a member of Congress. The issues included in this series cover the Trans-Pacific Partnership Act, the repeal of No Child Left Behind, the Highway and Transportation Funding Act, the Iran Sanctions Act, the Medicare Reform Act, repeal of the Affordable Care Act, and increasing the minimum wage to $12 per hour. Each item was presented with a brief explanation of the legislation, providing a useful measure of the policy preferences of respondents. We again measure policy positions on the legislation presented to respondents using binary indicators for respondents reporting they would vote in favor of the legislation. On the CCES, each policy was described as follows:

- *Trans-Pacific Partnership Act.* Free trade agreement among twelve Pacific nations (Australia, Brunei, Canada, Chile, Japan, Malaysia, Mexico, New Zealand, Peru, Singapore, and the United States).
- *Education Reform.* Repeals the No Child Left Behind Act, which required testing of all students and penalized schools that fell below federal standards. Allows states to identify and improve poor-performing schools.
- *Highway and Transportation Funding Act.* Authorizes $305 billion to repair and expand highways, bridges, and transit over the next five years.
- *Iran Sanctions Act.* Imposes new sanctions on Iran if Iran does not agree to reduce its nuclear program by June 30.
- *Accountability and Cost Reform Act.* Shifts Medicare from fee-for-service to pay-for-performance. Ties Medicare payments to doctors to quality-of-care measures. Requires higher premiums for seniors who make more than $134,000. Renews the Children Health Insurance Program (CHIP).
- *Repeal the Affordable Care Act.* Would repeal the Affordable Care Act of 2009 (also known as Obamacare).
- *Minimum Wage.* Raises the federal minimum wage to $12 an hour by 2020.

Budget Priorities

Budget priorities are measured at both the state and federal level. Relative trust between the federal and state government levels shapes public preferences for which level of government should be responsible for policy implementation (e.g., Leland et al., 2020). Given the polarization in the US federalist system (Goelzhauser & Konisky, 2020), understanding factors that shape budget priorities across levels of government is vital.

First, we examine budget priorities at the federal level in terms of addressing the budget deficit where respondents were asked whether the federal budget deficit should be resolved primarily through cuts to defense spending, cuts to domestic spending, or raising taxes. We create binary indicators for support for each preferred route to reducing the federal budget deficit.

Second, at the state level, in the post-election survey, we examine support for state government spending on several program areas. Respondents were asked to rate their support for state spending on welfare, health care, education, law enforcement, and transportation and infrastructure programs on a five-point scale ranging from greatly increase to greatly decrease. For ease of interpretation, we collapse these measures into binary indicators for respondents' support for slightly or greatly increasing state government spending in each of these policy areas.

Political Behaviors

Finally, we examine the link between PSM and a variety of political behaviors. Since PSM influences prosocial behaviors both within the workplace like organizational citizenship behavior (e.g., Boyd et al. 2018; Ingrams, 2020; Piatak & Holt, 2020b) and outside the workplace like volunteering (e.g., Christensen et al., 2015; Piatak, 2016a; Piatak & Holt, 2020), we ask: Are PSM-driven individuals also more politically engaged?

While some have examined how PSM and PSM-related values influence behaviors like voting (e.g., Holt, 2019) and, among councilmembers, seeking re-election (Ritz, 2015), scholars have noted a lack of PSM research on political positions and participation (Ritz, Brewer, & Neumann, 2016). In addition to voting, we examine more intensive forms of political participation, including working for a political campaign, attending local public meetings, putting up a political sign at their house, donating to a campaign, and considering running for office. The latter outcome, considering running for office, presents a particularly interesting outcome. While the PSM literature arose around considering the motivational base driving the behavior of those who enter the civil service, less attention has been paid to the theoretically equivalent role PSM may play in pursuing elected office.

2.4 Independent Variables

In the first part of our analysis, examining how PSM varies across different subgroups in Section 3, we focus on three sets of characteristics: demographics, socioeconomic status, and other motivating values systems. These later serve as control variables in Section 4 for our examination of PSM and public opinion.

2.4.1 Demographics and Individual Characteristics

Like most studies of the antecedents of PSM (e.g., Pandey & Stazyk, 2008; Parola et al., 2019), we begin with individual characteristics. While research has found women (Bright, 2005; Parola et al., 2019; Vandenabeele, 2011) and older Americans (Parola et al., 2019; Perry, 1997) tend to have higher levels of PSM, this literature is also filled with conflicting findings and null results (Ritz, Brewer, & Neumann, 2016), such as varying gender results when using the dimensional approach to PSM (Camilleri, 2007; DeHart-Davis, 2006). In addition, the literature is limited by the data available that tend to focus on binary gender and binary minority status, ignoring nuances across distinct racial and ethnic groups as well as LGBQ and transgender individuals.

We examine average levels of PSM across racial groups, by gender, and by sexuality. In the United States, demographic identities may shape PSM through differences in life experiences across groups. Racial minority groups may, through experiences with discrimination and prejudice, be more attuned to the value of public institutions and their role in ensuring a fairer and more just society. Similar experiences of social exclusion may also induce higher PSM among LGBTQ people. We measure demographics using self-reported survey responses from the preelection survey.

2.4.2 Socioeconomic Variables

Second, we estimate average differences in PSM across socioeconomic groups. While PSM research focuses on the role of education (e.g., Bright, 2005; Camilleri, 2007; Perry, 1997; Vandenabeele, 2011), we include education and several additional socioeconomic measures that not only provide individual resources but also socialization and social networks. For our purposes, we include educational attainment, income, employment status, and family status as measures of socioeconomic status.

We measure educational attainment with five categories: a high school diploma or less, some college, a two-year college degree, a four-year college degree, and a post-graduate degree. While PSM does not significantly affect the likelihood someone goes to college (Holt, 2018), educational experiences, such as coursework or service-learning opportunities, do significantly influence PSM (Seider et al., 2011; Holbein, 2017; Holt, 2019; Kim, 2020). Moreover, previous comparisons of samples of public sector employees have found, at a basic level, a positive link between education and PSM among those working in government (Bright, 2011).

We break household income into six categories ranging from less than $20,000 per year to $100,000 per year or more. We also compare those in the workforce, both full-time and part-time, those who are unemployed, and those who have left the workforce through retirement or disability. Finally, we compare average levels of PSM across groups with varying family commitments, such as those who are married or who have children. Family obligations, such as caring for children and ties to the labor market, may connect a person to community organizations and public services in ways that shape their PSM – regardless of their decision to work for public organizations. As with respondents' demographic information, their socioeconomic information was measured with self-reported survey items in the preelection wave of the survey.

2.4.3 Sociocultural Variables

Third, we look at the average levels of PSM across other group identities that also organize and motivate behavior through other values, such as religious affiliation, political ideology, and partisan affiliation. The literature on the antecedents of PSM consistently finds a positive link between religiosity and PSM among samples of public sector workers (Charbonneau & Van Ryzin, 2017; Perry, 1997). Meanwhile, research generally finds a negative link between PSM and conservative political ideologies (Charbonneau & Van Ryzin, 2017; Vandenabelee, 2011).

We use two survey items, developed by Pew Research, to measure religiosity. One asks respondents their religious identity and collapses the twelve original categories into six: Protestant, Mormon, Catholic, Muslim, Eastern Religions, no religion, and other religions. We also use the Pew survey item on religious service attendance, which asks respondents how often they attend religious services, as a measure of religiosity.

Finally, we examine differences in PSM along self-reported political ideology, using a five-category item ranging from very liberal to very conservative, and partisan identification, using self-reported political party registration.

2.4.4 Control Variables

In addition to the independent variables that make up the focus of our analyses, we include controls for additional economic status measures (home and stock ownership), labor market variables (union membership), and immigration (citizenship and generation) and military service status. We also include a common measure in political science, political interest, where respondents were asked the extent they follow government and public affairs on a four-point Likert scale from most of the time to hardly at all. Finally, we account for respondents' age alongside their other demographic information.

Table 2 summarizes the sample on a variety of observable characteristics, both overall and separately by those above average in PSM and those below average in PSM. The sample broadly reflects the demographic and socioeconomic distributions of the broader US population. Notably, the descriptive differences between low- and high-PSM individuals are relatively small and not significant on most characteristics. College graduates, Blacks, and Democrats are more likely to be high-PSM, while Asians are slightly less likely to be high-PSM. Otherwise, along income and labor market status, gender, and other racial groups, there's not a significant difference in the likelihood to be high-PSM versus low-PSM. Of course, a simple comparison of means may be misleading since many of these characteristics are correlated with each other. We lay out our analytic method for adjusting average PSM for other characteristics to better compare PSM-levels across groups in more apples-to-apples comparisons. Findings on factors corresponding to higher levels of PSM are discussed in Section 3.

Table 2 Summary of sample

	(1)	(2)	(3)
	All	Low PSM	High PSM
PSM	−0.00	−0.87***	0.72
	(1.00)	(0.64)	(0.58)
White	0.74	0.75	0.73
	(0.44)	(0.43)	(0.45)
Black	0.13	0.10*	0.14
	(0.33)	(0.30)	(0.35)
Latinx	0.07	0.07	0.07
	(0.25)	(0.26)	(0.25)
Asian	0.03	0.04*	0.02
	(0.17)	(0.19)	(0.14)
Native American	0.01	0.00	0.01
	(0.08)	(0.07)	(0.10)
Multiple race or other race	0.04	0.04	0.04
	(0.19)	(0.19)	(0.19)
Female	0.53	0.52	0.55
	(0.50)	(0.50)	(0.50)
Full-time employed	0.42	0.40	0.44
	(0.49)	(0.49)	(0.50)
Part-time employed	0.11	0.09	0.12
	(0.32)	(0.29)	(0.33)
Retired	0.19	0.21	0.18
	(0.39)	(0.41)	(0.38)
Student	0.06	0.05	0.06
	(0.23)	(0.22)	(0.24)
Unemployed	0.09	0.11*	0.07
	(0.28)	(0.31)	(0.26)
HH income < $20 K	0.11	0.12	0.10
	(0.31)	(0.32)	(0.30)
HH income > $100 K	0.17	0.15	0.18
	(0.38)	(0.36)	(0.39)
HS diploma or less	0.28	0.29	0.25
	(0.45)	(0.46)	(0.44)
College degree or more	0.38	0.34**	0.41
	(0.48)	(0.47)	(0.49)
Registered Democrat	0.39	0.29***	0.45
	(0.49)	(0.46)	(0.50)
Registered Republican	0.23	0.25	0.22
	(0.42)	(0.43)	(0.41)
Observations	1000	441	530

Note: Standard deviations in parentheses; the statistical significance of mean differences between low PSM and high PSM is tested using t-tests. *p < .10, **p < .05, and ***p < .01.

2.5 Methods

We use regression analysis to both compare average levels of PSM across the subgroups previously outlined and to examine the relationship between PSM and policy preferences, budget priorities, and political behaviors.

In Section 3, we present our results using the net effect of a variable of interest on PSM derived from our regression analysis using graphs to allow for an easier interpretation of our results. The bar graphs depict average PSM scores by a given variable after accounting for other factors. Higher bars reflect higher PSM scores and changes in PSM scores through the addition of controls to our regression models are visually represented by changes in bar height for a given variable. Regression output in tables with estimated coefficients and standard errors can be found in the Appendix.

In Section 4, we estimate linear probability models (LPM) that capture the average change in the likelihood of supporting a particular policy, legislation, budget change, or program associated with an increase of one standard deviation in an individual's PSM score. All inference from our analysis is made using heteroskedastic robust standard errors.

3 Who Has PSM?

Considering the many benefits of PSM, such as prosocial behavior both within and outside of the workplace, research has examined the antecedents of PSM (for reviews, see Pandey & Stazyk, 2008; Parola et al., 2019). However, much of this work has conflicting or null findings due to differences across PSM measures, samples, and country contexts. Most PSM research focuses on government employees, but this biases the sample to perhaps already high-PSM individuals. Using a national sample of US adults, we examine individual characteristics, socioeconomic factors, and other motivating values that influence levels of PSM.

3.1 Demographics and PSM

We begin our analysis by comparing average levels of PSM across racial, gender, and sexual orientation subgroups. Theoretically, demographic groups may differ in PSM through differential experiences with public organizations or other social experiences that may alter individuals' valuation of public institutions more broadly.

In Figure 1, the bars represent the net effect of race on PSM – the average PSM by subgroup after accounting for the effect of the control variables on PSM – and the shade of the bars reflects the controls included in the regression model used to calculate the net effect. Consistent with the summary statistics

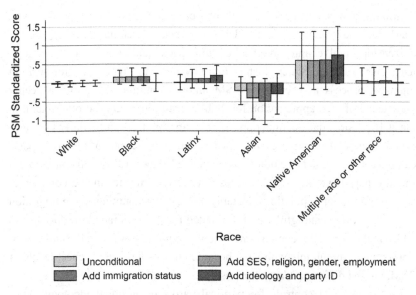

Figure 1 Average PSM by race, adjusted using OLS regression

Note: Caps on bars represent 95 percent confidence intervals of the net effect of race on PSM. Controls added iteratively as shown in the legend. N = 766.

presented previously, in Table 2, the lightest gray bars show that without any controls, there are relatively few statistically significant differences across groups. The difference between Blacks (0.15 standard deviations above the mean) and whites (0.03 standard deviations below the mean) is marginally significant ($p < 0.10$), while no other groups differ statistically from one another. Notably, however, Native Americans report high average PSM (0.63 standard deviations from the mean) but reflect such a small share of a nationally representative sample (less than 1 percent) that our estimates for their PSM are very imprecise.

The second, third, and fourth bars in each subgroup add all our controls, as described previously, to our regression models. Theoretically, these factors may be systematically associated with both race and PSM, so we aim to isolate average PSM attributable specifically to race by controlling for additional observed characteristics. Beginning with the second bar, we add controls for SES, gender, religion, and employment status. Note that even accounting for SES, gender, religion, and employment have little effect on estimated PSM by race – the Black-white gap in PSM shrinks slightly and becomes statistically insignificant as accounting for these differences increases the estimated average PSM among white people. Similarly, once we account for differences in SES, religion, employment status, and gender, average PSM among Latinx people increases while average PSM among Asians decreases.

Immigration status presents a theoretically ambiguous relationship with PSM. On the one hand, in the United States, overcoming the barriers to citizenship involves intensive background checks and testing on civic knowledge of the United States' history and government. Preparation for such an intensive process may cultivate PSM among immigrants through a deeper knowledge of, and appreciation for, public institutions. On the other hand, in the 2016 presidential election, opposition to immigration, particularly immigration from nonwhite countries, became a salient issue for one of the major party candidates. Increased prejudice and extended exposure to anti-immigration rhetoric may have undermined a desire to engage further in the community among immigrant populations. Notably, however, accounting for immigration status does not meaningfully alter estimated PSM across racial groups. As the tables in the Appendix demonstrate, relative to non-citizens and the children of immigrants, immigrants who have become citizens have the highest levels of PSM, but the differences are imprecisely estimated.

Finally, we add controls for political party and political ideology. After accounting for political affiliations and ideology, the Black-white gap in PSM shrinks to 0.02. Meanwhile, the estimated average PSM among Native Americans grows, and the difference between Native Americans and whites in PSM becomes marginally significant ($p<0.10$) – though we caution against over-interpretation, given the small number of Native Americans in a nationally representative sample. Finally, estimated levels of PSM among Latinx nearly doubles, and among Asians, it falls by nearly half. Overall, our results suggest that, overall, PSM does not significantly vary much by race and that differences across racial groups in political ideology and partisan affiliation explain some of the variation in PSM by race. Next, we conduct a similar analysis by gender and sexual orientation.

Figure 2 progresses in the same manner as Figure 1, exploring changes in average PSM scores across groups as controls enter the model. Notably, on average, cis women have higher PSM than cis men (0.16 versus –0.05), and the difference is statistically significant ($p < 0.05$) after accounting for all controls. As with Native Americans, LGBTQ Americans represent a proportionally small segment of the population, and as a consequence of their small sample size, we can only derive imprecise estimates of their PSM. Still, it appears transgendered males have a high average PSM, primarily explained by other related factors (e.g., SES, race, education, and political affiliation and ideology), while transgendered females have low PSM *after* accounting for all controls. Meanwhile, LGBQ respondents seem to have higher PSM than their heterosexual counterparts, but this gap shrinks to nearly zero after accounting for party identification and ideology. In other words, while cis men and women differ significantly on

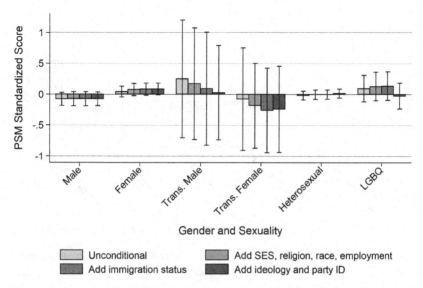

Figure 2 Average PSM by gender and sexual orientation, adjusted using OLS regression

Note: Caps on bars represent 95 percent confidence intervals of the net effect of race on PSM. Controls added iteratively as shown in the legend. N = 766.

PSM and this difference remains after accounting for other confounders, many of the differences in PSM between LGBTQ and heterosexual Americans can be explained primarily by systematic differences in political ideology.

3.2 Socioeconomic Status and PSM

We turn now to the link between socioeconomic status and PSM. Prior work on PSM, using samples of public sector employees, have found those with higher levels of education tend to report higher levels of PSM (Bright, 2005; Camilleri, 2007; Perry, 1997; Vandenabeele, 2011). The positive association between education and PSM might be through learning more about how our institutions work, experiences while in college, or simply a function of examining this association among those who join the public sector. We estimate the net effect of educational attainment on PSM in our national sample to see whether the relationship holds in the broader population after accounting for other factors.

A few patterns emerge from our analysis. First, in the broader public, only respondents with the highest levels of educational attainment (i.e., post-graduate degree holders) report significantly higher PSM than those with the lowest level of education (i.e., those with a high school diploma or less). However, after accounting for ideological and partisan differences between

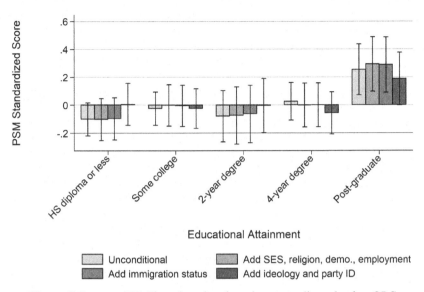

Figure 3 Average PSM by educational attainment, adjusted using OLS regression

Note: Caps on bars represent 95 percent confidence intervals of the net effect of race on PSM. Controls added iteratively as shown in the legend. N = 766.

those at the top and those at the bottom of educational attainment, the gap in PSM shrinks and is no longer statistically significant. Second, in terms of estimated average PSM, the differences between those with a high school diploma or less and those with educational attainment up to a four-year college degree are quite modest, particularly after accounting for political ideology and partisan differences. In light of the recent growth in polarization among whites, the demographic majority of the United States, by educational attainment (Harris, 2018) and growing partisan divide in views of higher education (Parker, 2019), this suggests that the previously established link between educational attainment and PSM may be due, in part, to a growing correlation between education and political ideology.

Household income, on the other hand, bears a more ambiguous relationship with PSM. Since much of the prior work has focused on samples of public or nonprofit sector employees, wages were largely reflective of rank due to the more pre-determined pay structure in the public sector. On the one hand, the growing correlation between educational attainment and income may also present a similar positive association between income and PSM, operating through some combination of education and political ideology. Similarly, those who have benefitted more from their community may feel a stronger

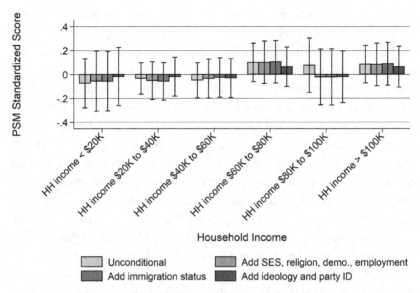

Figure 4 Average PSM by income bracket, adjusted using OLS regression

Note: Caps on bars represent 95 percent confidence intervals of the net effect of race on PSM. Controls added iteratively as shown in the legend. N = 766.

commitment to serving their community's need and interests. On the other hand, higher income may predispose individuals to devaluing community needs to minimize tax obligations.

In Figure 4, we present average PSM by income bracket. Notably, PSM does not seem to vary much by income bracket. In absolute terms, we observe higher PSM in middle to high-earning households and lower PSM in the lower-income brackets. However, the differences are never statistically significant across any groups and, after accounting for observable characteristics and political views, become quite small (about 0.10 of a standard deviation between the bottom and top brackets). Clearly, income plays a less systematic role in shaping PSM than other socioeconomic factors, such as education.

As noted previously, family ties and ties to the labor market also put people in touch with a variety of public institutions and community organizations. From arranging elder care for parents to attending court hearings for divorce proceedings to interacting with teachers, staff, and other parents at a child's school, family ties may yield more frequent interactions in public and community institutions that shape individuals' PSM. Similarly, even though public sector jobs often involve frequent contact with the general public, reliance on public infrastructure and services for commuting and operating businesses, and such experiences may also shape PSM.

Figures 5 and 6 estimate average PSM by family status and employment status, respectively. A few patterns emerge. First, holding all else constant, PSM does not differ significantly or substantively across marital status – with widows and widowers providing one potential exception. Given their small proportion in our sample (3.7 percent), our estimates of widowed respondents' PSM are imprecise and not statistically significant. That said, the point estimate reflects an average PSM score 0.35 standard deviations above the sample mean, a sizable average score. Experiencing the tragic loss of a loved one may trigger a recognition of the value and importance of broader community structures and supports and increase PSM in an on-going way. Still, our sample size limitations for this subgroup warrants caution in inferring too strong of a relationship from our estimates. Future work should examine the impact of experiences of loss on individuals' other-oriented values, such as altruism, PSM, and prosocial motivation more broadly.

Second, respondents with children report much higher PSM, on average, than those without children and this difference is statistically significant even after accounting for all the observable characteristics in our model. Respondents with at least one child score about 0.30 standard deviations higher on PSM than respondents without children, consistent with the possibility that caretaking responsibilities and contact with a variety of public and

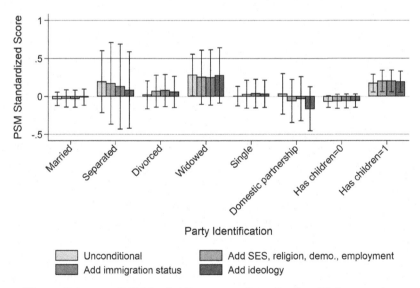

Figure 5 Average PSM by family status, adjusted using OLS regression

Note: Caps on bars represent 95 percent confidence intervals of the net effect of race on PSM. Controls added iteratively as shown in the legend. N = 766.

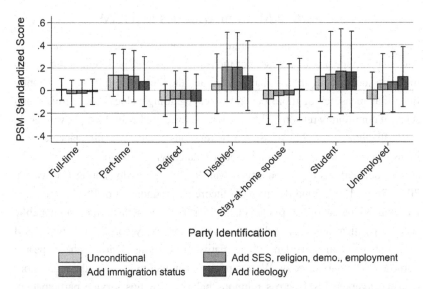

Figure 6 Average PSM by employment status, adjusted using OLS regression

Note: Caps on bars represent 95 percent confidence intervals of the net effect of race on PSM. Controls added iteratively as shown in the legend. N = 766.

community services for children underscores the importance of community service and public institutions for parents.

Regarding labor market status, the differences between full-time employees and others are generally small and statistically insignificant. After accounting for other observable factors in our model, part-time employees, students, and those who have left the labor market due to disability score higher, on average, than others; however, these differences are generally small (0.11 to 0.17 of a standard deviation higher than full-time employees), and none are statistically significant, which suggests that labor market status may matter less for individuals' PSM than the particular sector and occupation a person enters.

Collectively, our results suggest that many of the socioeconomic factors that appear associated with PSM in some prior work focusing on only public sector employees, such as income, family status, and educational status, carry a less systematic association in the broader public. Moreover, the stronger factors, such as educational attainment, appear to operate in part through political ideology and partisan identification, two factors that have been previously under-examined in the PSM literature. Finally, family experiences that bring people in contact with their broader community, such as having a child (and perhaps losing a spouse), are clearly positively associated with PSM, even after accounting for socioeconomic status, demographics, and political beliefs.

3.3 Other Motivating Values and PSM

The motivation to serve one's community and support the institutions that facilitate such service are, of course, not the only values and preferences that might motivate socially important behaviors. In fact, the literature on PSM consistently finds that measures of more general other-regarding values, like altruism and sense of community responsibility, are highly correlated with PSM (Nowell et al., 2016; Piatak & Holt, 2020a). Similarly, religious beliefs and attendance of religious services are regularly found to be correlated with PSM and entry into public service occupations (Charbonneau & Van Ryzin, 2017; Houston & Cartwright, 2007; Perry, 1997). Finally, given the theoretical foundation of PSM argues that individuals' valuation of public institutions motivates their interest in public service, political ideology and partisan affiliation likely corresponds with PSM to the extent that they overlap with normative dispositions regarding the scope and purpose of the public sector. We again use our model to estimate the regression-adjusted average PSM across religious beliefs, religious service participation, political ideology, and party identification.

As Figure 7 shows, we find little evidence that, in the general public, religious beliefs correspond with higher PSM. For instance, after controlling for all the variables in our model, including political identity variables, the average level of PSM reported by Protestants, Catholics, Mormons, and those with no religious

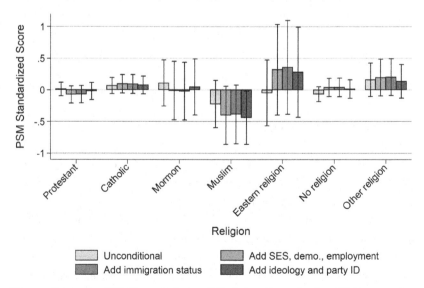

Figure 7 Average PSM by religious affiliation, adjusted using OLS regression

Note: Caps on bars represent 95 percent confidence intervals of the net effect of race on PSM. Controls added iteratively as shown in the legend. N = 766.

beliefs are all statistically indistinguishable from each other and relatively close in average PSM score. Meanwhile, respondents who identify as Muslim score below the sample average in PSM, and the difference is statistically significant. Respondents who identify with Eastern Religions (e.g., Buddhism, Hinduism, etc.) score fairly high in terms of PSM, but they are a small proportion of the population and sample, and consequently, we cannot be certain that their true average PSM levels are not equal to the national average.

Of course, the intensity with which one practices their religion may be the factor that also spills over into cultivating PSM. We use religious service attendance as a proxy for religious participation intensity to investigate the link between religiosity and PSM. In Figure 8, we present the estimated average PSM separately by respondents' reported frequency of religious service attendance (excluding weddings and funerals). Our results reveal that while religious identity itself does not predict PSM systematically or reliably, frequent participation in religious service does correspond significantly with PSM. After accounting for all other controls in our model, people who attend religious services weekly or more have, on average, higher PSM than those who never attend religious services and the difference is statistically significant. Moreover, those who attend religious services twice per week have average PSM scores about 0.37 standard deviations above the sample average, a substantively and statistically meaningful difference.

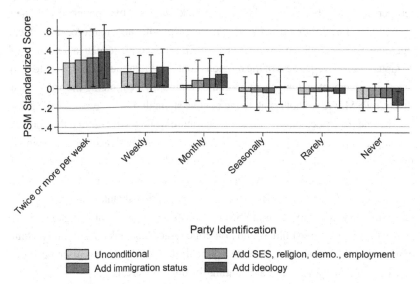

Figure 8 Average PSM by religious service attendance, adjusted using OLS regression

Note: Caps on bars represent 95 percent confidence intervals of the net effect of race on PSM. Controls added iteratively as shown in the legend. N = 766.

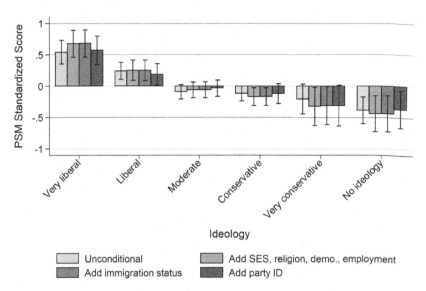

Figure 9 Average PSM by political ideology, adjusted using OLS regression

Note: Caps on bars represent 95 percent confidence intervals of the net effect of race on PSM. Controls added iteratively as shown in the legend. N = 766.

Together, the results suggest that religious practice, rather than a particular religious identity or belief system, explains the previously observed relationship between religious beliefs and PSM. The link suggests two potentially related possibilities. First, religious values may overlap with and reinforce the other-regarding values captured by measures of PSM. Second, regular attendance of religious services, regardless of the religious content or religious values, may lead to deeper involvement and engagement in the community, reinforcing the values that underpin PSM. We cannot speak to the relative strength of these potential mechanisms behind the association we observe, but future work could examine this further.

Our previous results regarding the link between PSM and race and educational attainment suggested a substantial association between political identity and PSM. For instance, after accounting for ideological and partisan differences by race, the difference between Blacks and whites in PSM shrank to approximately zero. Similarly, when examining PSM by educational attainment, the gap in PSM between college degree holders and non-college-goers shrank considerably. Both suggest that the values that animate political ideologies and that animate PSM may be correlated, even after accounting for other differences.

Figure 9 presents our estimates of average PSM score by self-reported ideology and confirms the association between political ideology and PSM. Specifically, both very liberal and liberal respondents score higher on PSM than conservative and very conservative respondents, and the differences are

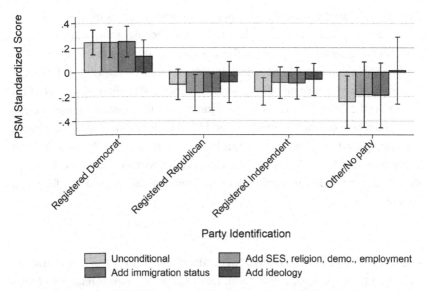

Figure 10 Average PSM by party registration, adjusted using OLS regression

Note: Caps on bars represent 95 percent confidence intervals of the net effect of race on PSM. Controls added iteratively as shown in the legend. N = 766.

statistically significant, even after accounting for all other factors. Given the association between liberalism and a philosophic preference for growth in the size and scope of the public sector in the United States, it is perhaps unsurprising that very liberal respondents score the highest in PSM (0.57 standard deviations above the sample mean) on average. Perhaps surprisingly, respondents who report no ideology score the lowest on PSM, and the difference is statistically significant. Together the results suggest PSM not only influences a drive to engage in public service, but also corresponds with individuals' philosophy about government more broadly. The low PSM scores among those who report no ideological disposition suggest that those lacking a consistent, self-aware view of the role of government in society may also be less motivated toward public service more generally. This suggests that some combination of philosophic disposition *and* knowledge of government generally plays an important role in shaping PSM in the broader public.

In Figure 10, we explore PSM by party registration. In recent decades, the major political parties in the United States have become more ideologically consistent internally and, thereby, more politically polarized (Doherty, 2014). Given our results that political ideology significantly predicts PSM, we might expect, as a result, that party affiliation would also be associated with PSM.

Figure 10 shows that the difference between parties in terms of PSM is similar to ideological divides, but the gap is smaller and becomes statistically insignificant after accounting for ideology. Together, the results suggest that the values captured by measures of PSM reflect, in part, normative views about the role of government rather than any group identity of party affiliation. As the political parties in the United States have become more ideologically consistent, the correlation between party registration and PSM is significant – until we account for ideology. After accounting for ideology, the estimated PSM scores for both Democrats and Republicans shrinks closer to the sample mean and becomes statistically insignificant. Further, they no longer significantly differ from one another.

3.4 Summary

Our analysis reveals a few patterns in the distribution of PSM across characteristics and life experiences. First, both race and gender appear related to PSM. Specifically, on average, Blacks have higher PSM than whites, and women have higher PSM than men. However, the Black-white gap in PSM disappears after accounting for ideology and partisan affiliation. Second, consistent with prior work, people who attend religious services (regardless of identification with a particular religion) and particularly high levels of education score higher in PSM. Finally, ideology and, to a lesser extent, party affiliation both significantly correlate with PSM. People who identify as liberals and Democrats, on average, score higher on PSM than conservatives and Republicans.

4 PSM and Public Opinion

Our results clearly show that political ideology and PSM are highly correlated and that the correlation between PSM and ideology explains many of the differences in PSM we observe across demographic and socioeconomic groups. Understanding the association between PSM and public opinion represents an important frontier in better understanding the nature of PSM. First, PSM advances understanding of public opinion, which plays a vital role in the policy making process. Second, PSM may more directly influence policy outcomes through the policy priorities of elected officials. Relatedly, through the decision making of public servants, the association between PSM and policy preferences can provide some indication of whether and how public servants might prefer government action to be directed on different issues. Lastly, for public administration and political science researchers, PSM may provide leverage in understanding who joins political campaigns, why they join, and how elected officials may better target messaging to appeal to those motivated to serve.

As previously described, we tackle the question of how PSM relates to public opinion using survey items that ask respondents about their support for policies in different issue areas, whether they would vote in favor of specific legislation if they were members of Congress, whether they support increased state government spending on a range of program areas, and political behaviors.

4.1 PSM and Policy Preferences

We begin by examining the relationship between PSM and support for specific policies discussed during the 2016 campaign on six issue areas: gun control, immigration, abortion and gay marriage, environmental regulations, criminal justice reform, and the budget deficit. As before, for ease of interpretation and clarity of presentation, we report our results using plots of the coefficient of interest (the effect of PSM on support) and confidence intervals used for hypothesis testing and statistical inference. In this section, we control for the full set of control variables, as described in Section 2, in all of our estimates.

We first look at the relationship between PSM and gun control policies included in the CCES preelection survey. The survey asked about four specific gun control policies that advocates or candidates have proposed during the 2016 campaign. First, respondents were asked about support for universal background checks on all sales of firearms, including guns sold at gun shows and over the Internet. Second, the survey asked respondents whether they supported a federal ban on state and local governments publishing the names and addresses of all gun owners. Third, the survey asked respondents whether they support bans on the sale and possession of assault rifles. Finally, respondents were asked whether they support policies that make it easier for people to obtain a concealed-carry permit, a permit that allows gun owners to carry a firearm in public hidden from view.

Figure 11 presents our estimates of the relationship between PSM and respondents' support for various gun control policy proposals considered by candidates or advocacy groups during the 2016 presidential campaign. For the first plot point in Figure 11, respondents were asked about their support for universal background checks on all gun purchases with no exceptions. Holding all else in the model constant, respondents who scored 1 standard deviation higher on our PSM measure than the average were 4 percentage points more likely to support universal background checks on all gun purchases, and this relationship was statistically significant. The second plot shows that, in contrast, there was no systematic relationship between PSM and support for preventing state and local governments from publishing the names and addresses of gun owners. Meanwhile, higher PSM is significantly associated with higher support for a ban on the sale and ownership of assault rifles and negatively associated with making concealed carry permits easier to obtain.

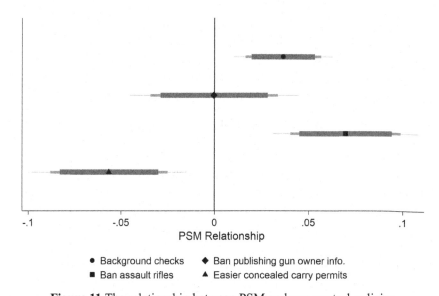

Figure 11 The relationship between PSM and gun control policies

Note: All controls are included in the model. Confidence intervals calculated using robust standard errors. 90 percent, 95 percent, and 99 percent confidence intervals are presented in descending order of line thickness.

A notable common theme in the relationships observed regarding PSM and gun control policy is the tendency toward a preference for direct government regulation of the gun market. PSM is positively related to government-mandated background checks, a policy aimed at ensuring a safer and more accountable market of gun buyers and sellers, and banning firearms believed to be less important for hobbyists or self-defense. That said, the pattern also reflects partisan and ideological views on gun control – both of which are also significant predictors in our model – and suggests that while PSM has an independent effect, the effect aligns with liberal ideological preferences as well. As we observed in Section 3, ideologically liberal respondents have, on average, higher levels of PSM. Given the trait-like stability of PSM (e.g., Holt, 2018; Witteloostuijn, Esteve, & Boyne, 2017; Wright, Hassan, & Christensen, 2017), the community-regarding orientation captured by PSM may lead to systematic sorting into ideological beliefs and partisan affiliation as well. On the other hand, ideological beliefs regarding the proper role of government may also induce PSM among adherents. Still, political ideology and PSM are not perfectly correlated, and at least some of the variation in policy preferences attributed to ideology actually operates through PSM.

If PSM relates to policy preferences in prioritizing direct government action toward public interest outcomes and service of community needs, environmental

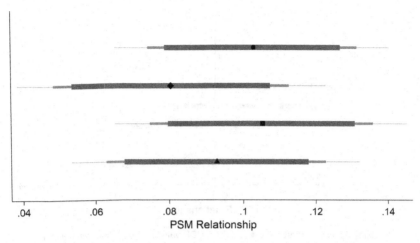

- ● EPA authority over Carbon emissions   ◆ Increase auto fuel efficiency standards
- ■ Require renewable energy minimum   ▲ Increase Clean Air and Water Act enforcement

Figure 12 The relationship between PSM and environmental policies

Note: All controls are included in the model. Confidence intervals calculated using robust standard errors. 90 percent, 95 percent, and 99 percent confidence intervals are presented in descending order of line thickness.

conservation represents a policy area likely to be strongly influenced by PSM. Environmental regulations often operate through industry standards mandated by the government, emissions limits, and delegated authority to the Environmental Protection Agency (EPA) to set and enforce standards and emissions limits. In Figure 12, we look at the link between PSM and support for Congress giving the EPA authority to regulate CO_2 emissions, changes to automobile standards to improve fuel efficiency, mandating a minimum amount of electricity that states must generate through renewable sources, and strengthening the enforcement of the Clean Air Act and Clean Water Act. Notably, all these policy positions involve the use of government regulatory and enforcement tools to impose some costs on industry and consumers toward the goal of achieving the public benefits of cleaner air and water and lower emissions of greenhouse gases.

Without exception, even after accounting for ideology and party affiliation, PSM significantly predicts support for all four of these environmental regulatory actions. Consistent with the possibility that people with high PSM have stronger preferences for policies that target broad community concerns over common resources and tools that involve government regulation of private actions that run counter to community needs, PSM has a particularly strong link to policy preferences regarding the regulation of industries in service of environmental conservation goals.

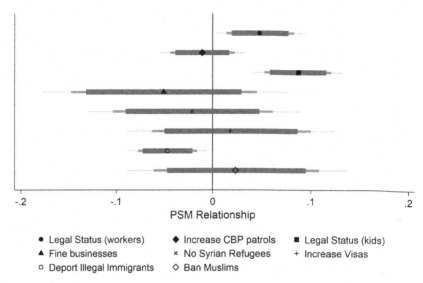

Figure 13 The relationship between PSM and immigration policies

Note: All controls are included in the model. Confidence intervals calculated using robust standard errors. 90 percent, 95 percent, and 99 percent confidence intervals are presented in descending order of line thickness.

In Figure 13, we turn to the relationship between PSM and policy preferences regarding regulating immigration into the US In the 2016 election, then-candidate Donald Trump centered his campaign on reducing immigration into the US through a mix of increased barriers to entry, increased deportation rates, and decreases in the number of visas made available to immigrants. Consequently, immigration policy became a salient and highly ideological policy area heading into the election.

Broadly, the policy preferences surveyed on immigration deal with granting legal rights and protections to currently undocumented immigrants (those who work and pay taxes for at least three years and those brought to the US as children), increased government enforcement of immigration laws, and decreasing the inflow of immigrants to the country. Theoretically, PSM relates, in part, to protecting the rights of others; however, PSM is often conceptualized as deriving utility from actions that benefit a particular community or institution with which a person identifies. The transference of motivating values captured in measures of PSM to noncitizens remains less clear. On the one hand, the importance of basic rights of others often included in measures of PSM may operate to include immigrants. On the other hand, immigrants may fall into an out-group, not reflected in motivations to serve one's community.

In Figure 13, the policy preferences associated with PSM suggests two things. First, PSM has a significant, positive relationship with policies aimed at granting basic rights of noncitizens and a significant negative relationship with policies aimed at abridging basic rights. For instance, the first plot in Figure 13 shows that a 1 standard deviation increase in PSM corresponds with a 5 percentage-point increase in the likelihood a person supports granting legal status to currently undocumented immigrants in the US who have worked and paid taxes for 3 years or more without a felony conviction. The same PSM change is associated with an even larger 9 percentage-point increase in the probability of support for granting legal status to undocumented immigrants brought to the US as children. Finally, those with high PSM are about 5 percentage points *less* likely to support deporting undocumented immigrants. All three of these policies share a thread of granting basic rights to immigrants living in and contributing to communities throughout the US

Second, PSM does not significantly affect support for policies aimed at curbing immigration now or in the future. While support for banning immigrants from Muslim nations, refusing refugees from the conflict in Syria, and increasing the number of US Customs and Border Patrol agents patrolling the US-Mexico border significantly differs by ideology (see Appendix Table A4), the association with PSM is small and not significantly different from zero. Collectively, the results are consistent with PSM mapping onto both basic rights as an important public interest to be upheld and bounding one's motivating values to a particular community. For instance, the burden of the policies for increasing patrols on the US-Mexico border or altering the rules surrounding which immigrants to accept in the future falls onto people not yet within US territory and not yet members of the broader national community. At least regarding immigration policy, PSM does not seem to shape policy preferences when the target population falls outside a broad definition of the current community population.

The right to continue living and contributing to the community you work and pay taxes in (or were brought to as a child) without the fear of deportation to another country represents a rather basic right. However, other legal, Constitutional rights, such as a right to an abortion or the right to marriage regardless of sexual orientation, have been a matter of ideological debate for decades. Moreover, given the link between participation in religious services and PSM and the divide on family planning and sexual orientation issues along religious lines, the theoretical link between PSM and Constitutional rights on these issues is ambiguous and puts concern for the rights of others core to PSM in tension with religious views on access to abortion and sexual orientation.

Figure 14 shows our estimates of the link between PSM and policy preferences regarding the right to abortion, contraceptives, and homosexuals' right to marry.

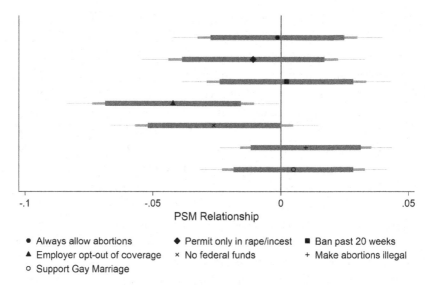

Figure 14 The relationship between PSM and family planning and marriage policies

Note: All controls are included in the model. Confidence intervals calculated using robust standard errors. 90 percent, 95 percent, and 99 percent confidence intervals are presented in descending order of line thickness.

Perhaps unsurprisingly, PSM does not systematically shape many of the policies that affect the Constitutional right to an abortion or for homosexuals being allowed to marry. These policy positions are strongly and significantly shaped by ideology, partisan affiliation, and religiosity. However, there are two exceptions to this rule. People with high PSM scores are significantly less likely to support a policy allowing employers to opt out of abortion coverage in their employer-provided insurance plans. People with a high PSM are also less likely to support a prohibition of federal funds being used to support any abortion services, though this relationship is only marginally significant ($p < 0.10$). One possibility may be that people with high PSM take a strong view against allowing discrimination in access to otherwise Constitutionally defined legal rights. That is, while religious or ideological views may dominate the question of whether abortion and gay marriage *should* be Constitutionally protected rights, PSM may shape whether someone views employer or fiscal denial of Constitutionally protected rights as unacceptable. Of course, our data limitations preclude our ability to investigate this question further or with more rigor so we caution readers to view this as one possibility that must be examined in more depth in future work.

PSM may also shape views regarding the enforcement of the law and punishment of violations of the law. After a string of police-involved deaths

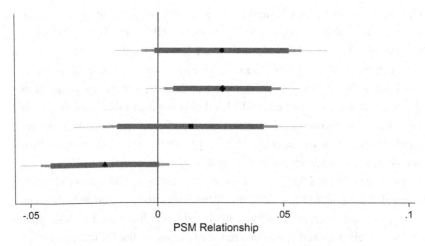

Figure 15 The relationship between PSM and criminal justice policies

Note: All controls are included in the model. Confidence intervals calculated using robust standard errors. 90 percent, 95 percent, and 99 percent confidence intervals are presented in descending order of line thickness.

in 2014, including the shooting deaths of Michael Brown (eighteen years old) and Tamir Rice (twelve years old) and the choking death of Eric Garner (forty-four years old), the issue of police use-of-force and accountability rose in salience in national politics. In the 2016 campaign, criminal justice reform measures, such as eliminating mandatory minimum sentencing requirements for drug-related offenses or requiring police officers to wear body cameras to ensure accountability for actions taken on duty, were often considered by candidates alongside more conventional policy measures like increasing police presence and raising the penalties for felony offenses when the offender has prior convictions. Respondents were surveyed about their support for these four policy proposals in the CCES.

Given a core concern with rights and the public interest undergirding PSM, the link between PSM and policy preferences on criminal justice issues remains theoretically ambiguous. On the one hand, PSM may lead people to support policies intended to protect the rights of individuals accused of a crime. On the other hand, PSM may drive support of policies that provide additional resources to police to keep communities safe and reduce crime.

Figure 15 plots the relationship between PSM and policy preferences for criminal justice policies salient during the 2016 presidential campaign. Relative to policies in other areas, the association between PSM and policy preferences on criminal justice issues is smaller and generally not statistically distinguishable from 0. However, people with higher levels of PSM are slightly more likely to support requiring police officers to wear body cameras while on duty than their otherwise similar peers. The small and insignificant relationship between PSM and either decreasing or increasing sentencing stringency suggests that PSM does not speak to views on the level of punishment that criminals should face above and beyond political ideology and partisanship. In contrast, the more administrative policy of strengthening the possibility of holding police officers accountable for misconduct or violating the rights of community members does seem to be associated with PSM, even beyond ideology and partisanship.

Finally, heading into the 2016 presidential election, Congress had recently passed or was currently considering legislation that became flash points during the election and spoke to a range of issues. In the CCES, respondents were asked how they would vote on each of these bills if they were members of Congress. The question aims at eliciting policy preferences of individuals salient enough that they would act on their preferences if given the authority to do so. The bills included in the sequence asked of respondents touched on international affairs, such as the Tran-Pacific Partnership Act (TPP) and the Iran Sanctions Act; health care, such as the Medicate Accountability and Cost Reform Act and the Repeal of the Affordable Care Act; and domestic issues, such as education reform, infrastructure spending, and raising the federal minimum wage to $12.

Figure 16 plots our estimated relationship between PSM and respondents' likelihood to vote in favor of each item on the Congressional agenda. Two patterns emerge immediately. First, consistent with the theoretical link between PSM and a value-preference for aid to a particular community, the bills that involve international affairs have a much weaker relationship with PSM. Support for the TPP, a trade deal that would set rules, regulations, and standards around trade between the United States and many nations in the Pacific region of the world (Japan, New Zealand, Australia, Brunei, Malaysia, Singapore, Vietnam, Peru, Chile, Mexico, and Canada) has a small, positive, marginally significant relationship with PSM. Meanwhile, PSM does not significantly influence support for the Iran Sanctions Act, an amendment to the 1996 law that imposed economic sanctions on companies that do business with Iran to curtail the Iranian government's pursuit of nuclear arms. Together, the results are consistent with our observations regarding the link between PSM and immigration policy – PSM seems to influence preferences for policies targeted at a community to which one belongs. PSM does not seem to affect policy preferences beyond ideology and partisanship for policies providing only indirect effects on the community one aims to serve.

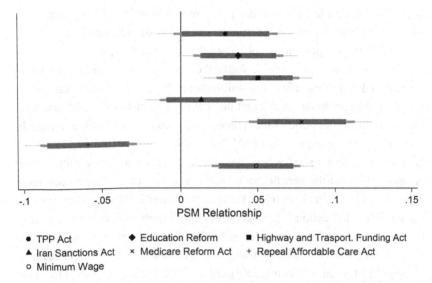

Figure 16 The relationship between PSM and support for items on the congressional agenda

Note: All controls are included in the model. Confidence intervals calculated using robust standard errors. 90 percent, 95 percent, and 99 percent confidence intervals are presented in descending order of line thickness.

Second, PSM strongly shapes policy preferences on policies that direct spending to aid domestic communities. For instance, holding all else constant, people with high PSM were 8 percentage points more likely to support the Medicare Reform Act, a bill aimed at renewing the Child Health Insurance Program, raising the Medicare contribution asked of wealthier households, and linking Medicare payments to health outcomes rather than services to disincentivize the prescription of unneeded tests and services. Meanwhile, high-PSM individuals were significantly less likely to support repealing the Affordable Care Act, the law passed under President Obama in 2010 that increased regulations on health insurance companies, expanded eligibility and funding for Medicaid, and provided a variety of subsidies for purchasing health insurance.

Beyond a policy preference for health care access, PSM has a positive and significant relationship with support for increasing the federal minimum wage to $12 per hour, as then presidential candidate Hillary Clinton proposed, and passing the Highway and Transportation Funding Act, which would spend $305 billion on bridge and highway repair and expansion. The last domestic bill surveyed, education reform, involved repealing the No Child Left Behind Act to undo the link between standardized test scores and federal aid for schools. PSM also had a positive, significant relationship with supporting the education reform bill considered, but the effect was slightly smaller.

Collectively, the patterns we observe between PSM and policy preferences points to two points of emphasis for further theoretical and empirical development of PSM work. First, the link between PSM and policy preferences varies by the beneficiary and target population. For instance, PSM generally has a weaker link to policies that relate to other countries or communities. In short, this pattern suggests that PSM likely shapes individuals' views contingent on the point of reference the individual takes as representing their "community" and the beneficiary of public service. The referent-contingent nature of PSM might also explain the apparent lower PSM we observe among conservatives in Section 3. Conservatives may simply define their communities and objects of service differently than liberals and in a manner not captured by commonly used measures of PSM. Future research could examine whether PSM, even with commonly used measures, predicts support for some policies targeted at communities and recipients, with a positive valence among conservatives but not liberals (and vice versa) that is not captured in the policies examined here.

Second, consistent with early ideas about fairness, benevolence, and representation of community interests serving as pillars of responsible administration in a democratic government (e.g., Frederickson, 1997; Gooden, 2015; Mosher, 1968; Perry & Rainey, 1988), PSM seems to most strongly affect policies that restrict or enhance established rights among community members. For instance, PSM significantly predicts opposition to deportation and support for granting legal rights to immigrants. Similarly, PSM is unrelated to support for abortion and gay marriage, but significantly correlates with opposition to restrictive policies on abortion, such as employer coverage opt-outs or barring federal funds for abortion and contraceptive services. These patterns suggest that PSM does not affect broad philosophic debates regarding which immigrants should be allowed to enter the country or whether abortion or gay marriage should be allowed independently of ideology. However, even accounting for ideology, restrictions on existing rights seem to be opposed by higher-PSM individuals. Recall that while average PSM on our more conventional measure of PSM is higher among liberals, a still sizable proportion of high-PSM individuals are Republicans. Thus our results are identifying issues salient among high-PSM individuals across party and ideological lines. As such, high-PSM individuals clearly place a higher value on equal application of the law and access to legal rights for vulnerable communities. We believe the future exploration of this boundary of PSM would be a productive and interesting area of further inquiry.

4.2 PSM and Budget Priorities

Of course, policy preferences alone do not tell the full story. As former vice president Joe Biden said in 2008, "Don't tell me what you value. Show me your budget, and I'll tell you what you value." Competing budgetary priorities play a perpetual role in all elections and conversations on public policy. Toward that end, the CCES asked respondents two items related to budgetary priorities. The first asked respondents how they would prefer the US deals with the federal budgetary deficit. The second asks respondents whether state governments should increase or decrease spending on programs related to welfare, education, health care, infrastructure, and law enforcement.

Figures 17 and 18 present our estimates of the relationship between PSM and respondents' positions on fiscal issues at both the federal and state levels. First, as Figure 17 shows, PSM does not shape preferences for cutting domestic or defense spending or raising revenue as a means to deal with the federal budget deficit beyond ideology or partisan affiliation. Second, Figure 18 suggests strong preferences for increased state government spending on programs in all policy areas, even after accounting for ideology and partisanship. PSM is most strongly related to increased state-level spending on education; however, there is a large, positive, and statistically significant

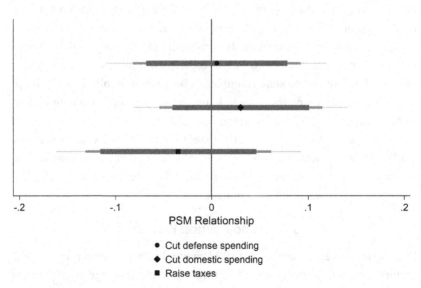

Figure 17 The relationship between PSM and federal deficit solutions

Note: All controls are included in the model. Confidence intervals calculated using robust standard errors. 90 percent, 95 percent, and 99 percent confidence intervals are presented in descending order of line thickness.

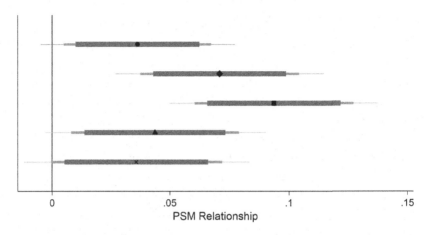

Figure 18 The relationship between PSM and state spending priorities

Note: All controls are included in the model. Confidence intervals calculated using robust standard errors. 90 percent, 95 percent, and 99 percent confidence intervals are presented in descending order of line thickness.

relationship between PSM and support for increased spending on health care, law enforcement, and welfare programs, as well. The relationship between PSM and support for state spending on infrastructure projects is the weakest, though still positive and marginally significant. On the one hand, the theoretical link between the desire to serve the public makes the relationship between PSM and more state resources to be given to public services intuitive and sensible. Of course, this link may reflect a response among higher-PSM people to decades of privatization and increased contracting out of public services. On the other, to the extent high-PSM individuals sort into public sector positions, the link raises the possibility that budget maximizing behavior posited long ago (e.g., Niskannen, 1976) might occur if not checked elsewhere in the system of government.

4.3 PSM and Political Behaviors

Finally, in the same manner that PSM may influence selection into public sector jobs and volunteering, PSM might provide leverage in explaining variation in engagement in the political sphere of public service, such as voting, joining a campaign, or running for office. In the post-election survey, the CCES asked respondents whether they participated in a variety of campaign-related behaviors (e.g., voting, attending local community

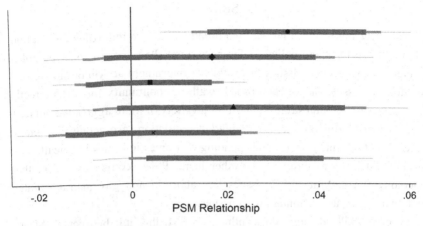

Figure 19 The relationship between PSM and political engagement

Note: All controls are included in the model. Confidence intervals calculated using robust standard errors. 90 percent, 95 percent, and 99 percent confidence intervals are presented in descending order of line thickness.

meetings, putting up campaign signs, working for a campaign). In addition, in the preelection survey, the CCES asked participants whether they considered running for office. We use these measures to estimate the association between PSM and engaging in a variety of political behaviors.

While PSM is associated with civic engagement, like volunteering, there is not as strong of a relationship with political engagement. In political science, political interest is often used to assess levels of political knowledge (e.g., Dancey & Sheagley, 2013; Dolan & Hansen, 2020) and political ambition (see Holman & Schneider, 2018, for a discussion of concerns with the supply-side approach). Prior (2010) argues, "Political interest is typically the most powerful predictor of political behaviors that make democracy work" (747).

As shown in Figure 19, we find PSM significantly increases public meeting attendance and intent to run for an elected position. While political interest also significantly corresponds to these behaviors as well as working for and donating to a campaign and voting, we find it interesting both political interest and PSM correspond to attending public meetings and political ambition. Perhaps PSM taps into a desire to participate in advancing government institutions and operations in addition to following public affairs.

4.4 Summary

Collectively, our results highlight two broad takeaways regarding the relationship between PSM and policy preferences. First, PSM seems to shape policy preferences strongly on issues that involve government action or intervention on domestic issues that affect a broad swath of community members directly. For instance, we found strong support for a variety of more aggressive environmental and gun market and labor market regulation, protecting immigrants already in the United States, and spending on domestic issues like health care access and infrastructure. On the other hand, PSM seems less salient than ideology and partisanship on issues like abortion and gay marriage, international affairs, and criminal justice issues.

Second, while ideology does influence PSM, the link between PSM and policy preferences suggests that some issues are more salient ideologically, while others speak to PSM more directly. More importantly, PSM seems to have effects on policy preferences that operate distinctly from ideology and partisanship. As we showed in Section 3, there is a significant link between PSM and ideology. One interpretation of that association could be that PSM captures a dimension of ideological commitments. Alternatively, given changes in ideological sorting across parties and growing party polarization, the link between PSM and ideology observed in Section 3 may be the result of members of the public motivated to serve the public interest sorting into partisan and ideological camps that support government action more broadly, as support for government action itself has become a partisan and ideological issue.

We lack the longitudinal data necessary to disentangle these possibilities; however, if PSM merely captured a dimension of ideology, when examining policy issues salient to a polarized election and associated with partisan and ideological positions, we would expect PSM to be absorbed by ideology or partisan affiliation. We show that on many policy issues, PSM provides explanatory power beyond ideology and partisanship. Indeed, one potential theory to explain contemporary legislative gridlock and aversion to bipartisan compromise is that the values captured by measures of PSM previously overlapped some portion of the two major US parties and is now underrepresented in the conservative party.

5 Discussion

With increasing polarization in politics and across aspects of our society as well as declining confidence in government and social capital, could PSM be a helpful lens to understand individual differences, policy preferences, and political behaviors? PSM represents a predisposition toward the betterment of society, based on public institutions. PSM research grew out of research on public/private differences (e.g., Perry & Rainey, 1988) and government career preferences (e.g., Perry & Wise, 1990) but has expanded. PSM corresponds to a range of benefits in employee behavior (e.g., Boyd et al., 2018; Piatak & Holt, 2020a), for organizational outcomes (e.g., Andersen, Heinesen, & Pedersen, 2014; Bellé, 2013), and for the community through broader service outside of the workplace (e.g., Piatak & Holt, 2020b). Given the benefits of PSM, we examine who has PSM and how PSM influences public opinion, policy preferences, and political behaviors. If PSM shapes values and preferences, it would play an important role in shaping public policy and outcomes.

PSM may shape policy making both indirectly and directly through public opinion policy preferences and priorities. Following the New Deal in response to the Great Depression and World War II, the role of government has expanded to address societal problems. More recently, following the September 11th terrorist attacks, the Great Recession of 2007–2009, and the COVID-19 pandemic, Roberts (2020) asserts the government has become the ultimate bearer of risk. As such, despite declining levels of trust and confidence (e.g., Cole & Kincaid, 2000; Jennings, 1998; Leland et al., 2020), public demands of government have been rising. Understanding the priorities and preferences of public opinion may shape policy agendas, options, and outcomes.

Public opinion plays a key role in the policy process. Public problems, issues, and preferences are often at the heart of agenda-setting theories on how issues and policy alternatives rise in and fall out of both the public's and policy makers' attention. The prominent role of public opinion can be seen in agenda-setting and policy process theories from the issue-attention cycle (Downs, 1972), to explaining periods of stability and change (Baumgartner & Jones, 2010), to the opening of policy windows (Kingdon, 1995), to the role of symbols, values, and shared meanings (Stone, 1988), to a prominent external factor in the advocacy coalition framework (Sabatier & Weible, 2007), to social contagion to explain policy diffusion (e.g., Pacheco, 2012). Whether to elevate individual private problems to the agenda or to illustrate public support for a policy proposal, public opinion shapes the policy agenda, options, and outcomes.

More directly, PSM may shape the policy making and decision-making of public officials, policy makers, and bureaucrats. Across levels of the organizational hierarchy, employees have a certain amount of discretion from government leaders and policy makers to street-level bureaucrats. The preferences and priorities of public leaders may shape their policy and administrative agendas and form the basis of the organization's culture (e.g., Pandey et al., 2016; Stazyk, Davis & Portillo, 2017). Street-level bureaucrats also play a policy-making role as they have wide discretion in the allocation of benefits or sanctions in their direct interactions with citizens (Lipsky, 2010). Frontline employees may break or bend rules for a variety of reasons (e.g., Borry & Henderson, 2020; Piatak, Mohr, & McDonald, 2020). As such, scholars call for shared norms in public service to guide administrative decision-making (e.g., Friedrich, 1940; Mosher, 1982; Roberts, 2019a; Young, Wiley, & Searing, 2020). Frederickson (2015), who put forth social equity as a pillar of public administration, argues: "Administrative discretion is harnessed to the public good not by more rules but by appreciation of the spirit of the law and its relation to the public good" (66). PSM might shape individual priorities and preferences providing a common basis for administrative decision-making.

For these reasons, we examine who has PSM in Section 3 and how PSM influences public opinion in Section 4. Here, we discuss the key findings from each section along with future research directions and implications.

5.1 Antecedents of PSM

Research has examined the antecedents of PSM (for a review, see Pandey & Stazyk, 2008). Since PSM research tends to focus on the public sector, much of this work uses government surveys or is based on samples of government employees. However, this raises several issues. First, many examine how organizations can inhibit or enhance PSM among their employees (for a meta-analysis, see Harari et al., 2017). We know much less about how *individual* characteristics and factors correspond to PSM. Second, using samples of government employees to examine predictors of PSM is problematic. People driven by PSM are more likely to work in the public sector (e.g., Asseburg & Homberg, 2020). Therefore, samples of government employees will be biased toward already having higher levels of PSM than a more general sample of the population. Third, much of this work is based on government surveys that limit the information gathered. For example, government surveys do not include questions about sociocultural factors, like political ideology and religiosity. In addition, publicly available data often limits analyses of gender and race to binary categories. With data neglecting to capture the full diversity of individuals and factors that may shape PSM, we have an incomplete picture of PSM determinants.

To address these concerns, we draw upon a novel module of the CCES, a cooperative political science survey surrounding the 2016 US presidential election. We build upon research on PSM antecedents by examining additional demographic, socioeconomic, and sociocultural factors, such as sexuality, race and ethnicity, immigration status, religion, religiosity, and political views.

Women have significantly higher levels of PSM than men. We find identifying as a woman positively influences PSM, while identifying as a man negatively influences PSM. This is in line with past work (Bight, 2005; Parola et al., 2019; Vandenabeele, 2011) and research on gender differences across PSM dimensions (Camilleri, 2007; DeHart-Davis et al., 2006). Riccucci (2018) suggests genetics as well as contextual or environmental factors underlie the link between gender and PSM. In addition to binary gender differences, we find transgendered males have high average PSM, while transgender females have low average PSM. While gender is, in part, socially construed and often the most salient social identity (Jenkins, 2014), gender is also biological. Much like Christensen, Moon, and Whitford (2020) find evidence of a genetic basis in job sector selection, our finding that cis women as well as transgender males have high average PSM illustrates that gender has both a biological and social influence on PSM. The biological influence also supports the notion that PSM is a predisposition rather than a fluid state.

Race matters. Unlike prior work that neglects to find any relationship between race and PSM (Bright, 2005; Charbonneau & Van Ryzin, 2017), we find significant differences in average PSM across racial groups. Black individuals have a higher average PSM than white individuals, but this dissipates after controlling for political ideology and party. Interestingly, the average PSM for Latinx individuals is higher in our fullest models. Meanwhile, Native Americans have relatively high PSM, and Asians have relatively low PSM on average. While some of these groups are small for precise estimates, the differences in average PSM across racial groups illustrates that the relationship between race and PSM is more nuanced than nonexistent. Much like PSM varies across country cultures (e.g., Kim, 2015; Vandenabeele & Van de Walle, 2008), different racial norms, beliefs, and traditions likely shape PSM.

The PSM link to education may be a matter of politics. We find only those with the highest level of education, a post-graduate degree, have higher PSM compared to those with less than a high school diploma. Despite past research finding education to be a primary predictor of PSM (Bright, 2005; Camilleri, 2007; Pandey & Stazyk, 2008; Perry, 1997; Vandenabeele, 2011), education is not significant in our fullest models. While education is a resource and may play a role in socialization, education is political (e.g., Meier, Stewart, & England, 1989; Thomas, 2016) and polarizing (e.g., Houston, 2019). Higher education has roots in colonialism, including the field of public administration (Roberts, 2019b). Even today, we see political efforts to maintain the whiteness of higher education, such as the US Department of Justice (DOJ) targeting lawsuits against universities with affirmative action, including Harvard and Yale (e.g.,

DOJ, 2020; Simmons, 2019). Our findings suggest politics play a greater role than educational attainment.

Having children and life experiences influence PSM rather than resources. We find people with children and who have lost their spouse have higher levels of PSM, while there is little connection to income. Since most PSM research focuses on a sample of government or nonprofit sector employees, we know little about how household income may relate to PSM. While Perry (1997) found income has a negative influence on PSM, we find higher-income households have higher average PSM, but this is largely due to education and political ideology, as PSM is not significantly influenced by income level (nor proxies like whether respondents are homeowners or stockholders) in our fullest models.

People with children have significantly higher levels of PSM compared to those without children. Our work aligns with Camilleri (2007), who found that people married with children have higher PSM using the dimensional approach. Perhaps having children moves people into a caring, other-oriented role; expands one's social network and interaction with public institutions, including schools; or enhances one's desire to leave the world a better place. Based on social learning theory (Bandura, 1971), parents may role-model PSM and other-oriented values and behaviors in raising their child(ren). For example, Stritch and Christensen (2016) find parent volunteering influences the likelihood of adult children volunteering, except for fathers and daughters, in addition to a direct link between PSM and volunteering. Social networks also build social capital (e.g., Coleman, 1988; Putnam, 2000), where children may bring weak ties into an individual's life and new social circles (Granovetter, 1973). As such, people with children often receive invitations to engage in service such as volunteering at a child's school, chaperoning a class trip, or serving on a parent-teacher board that may enhance PSM. Lastly, much like PSM work has drawn upon Erickson (1963) generativity to explain why PSM tends to increase with age (e.g., Pandey & Stazyk, 2008), people with children may care more about making the world a better place for future generations.

Widow(er)s stand out as having higher average PSM when examining marital status, and this status remains significant in our fullest models. Perhaps the life experience of losing a loved one and the supports needed to cope with such trauma enhance community ties and PSM. Despite research that finds widows and widowers have the lowest volunteer rates (Musick & Wilson, 2008), volunteering reduces loneliness and (re)connection with children, as well as friends, and the community partially compensates for their loss (Carr & Utz, 2020). Widows face a great deal of emotional labor (e.g., Ben-Asher & Bokek-

Cohen, 2020; Pearl, 2020), in addition to coping with grief. Many support groups and programs are aimed at helping those who lose a spouse that may expand one's social network and community connections. According to socio-emotional selectivity theory (Carstensen, 1992), people become increasingly selective in how they spend their time, investing time and effort into emotionally meaningful tasks. People may focus their efforts on meaningful public service following a major loss, like the death of a spouse.

Occupation or job sector may shape PSM rather than employment status. Across employment status categories, we find slightly higher PSM among part-time employees, students, and those who left the labor market due to a disability, but these differences are not significant in our fullest models. Since PSM grew out of examinations of public/private differences (e.g., Perry & Rainey, 1988; Perry & Wise, 1990) and PSM corresponds to government employment (e.g., Clerkin & Coggburn, 2012; Holt, 2018; Piatak, 2016a; Stritch & Christensen, 2016; Vandenabeele, 2008b; Wright, Hassan, & Christensen, 2017), job sector, or occupation (Andersen et al., 2011; Kjeldson, 2014; Kjeldson & Jacobsen, 2013) may predict PSM more than one's employment status.

Religiosity influences PSM as may religious beliefs. We find individuals with greater religiosity, measured by church attendance, have higher levels of PSM compared with those who are not religious or rarely attend church. This corresponds to past research finding PSM increases with religious activities (Perry et al., 2008), family religiosity (Charbonneau & Van Ryzin, 2017), and religiosity (Witteloostuijn et al., 2017). Church may play a socialization role in terms of instilling certain values, beliefs, and traditions, and may play a role in expanding one's social network and ties. We also find that religious beliefs may correspond to PSM with higher average PSM among Eastern religions and lower average PSM among those identifying as Muslim. Much like race and ethnicity, religion likely brings certain norms that may shape individual values and orientations to the world, public service, and government institutions.

PSM is political. We find significant differences in PSM by both political ideology and political party identification. Unfortunately, like many issues in the United States today, PSM is (or has become) partisan. People identifying as very liberal have significantly higher average PSM, while people identifying as a Republican or Independent decreases PSM. Much like Charbonneau and Van Ryzin (2017) find being raised in a conservative family decreases PSM and Vandenabelee (2011) finds lower levels of PSM among the extreme right, we find conservative ideology and party are associated with lower levels of PSM.

PSM is (or may have become) political with the increasing political polarization in the United States. Growing political polarization both reduces trust in government (e.g., Banda & Kirkland, 2018; Hetherington & Rudolph, 2015) and has increasingly polarized the public by party (e.g., Iyengar, Sood, & Lelkes, 2012; Simas, Clifford, & Kirkland, 2020). With this deepening division by ideology and political party, concern for the public grounded in public institutions does not currently seem like a common goal. This is not to say conservatives have no concern for helping others. Piatak and Holt (2020a, 2020b) find no significant political differences in organizational citizenship behavior, volunteering, or blood donation. Moreover, in Table 2, we see that 22 percent of high-PSM individuals in our sample are registered Republicans – a clear indication that PSM and conservatism are not irreconcilable. However, the desire to help others rooted in public institutions may have become more partisan. We lack a sufficiently large sample to further investigate policy differences between high- and low-PSM individuals *within* each party, but we believe future research in this vein would be fruitful.

People with higher levels of political interest also have higher levels of PSM. Political interest, a common measure in political science, asks the degree to which individuals follow public affairs, which tends to correspond to political knowledge (e.g., Dancey & Sheagley, 2013; Dolan & Hansen, 2020) and political behaviors (e.g., Prior, 2010). Unsurprisingly, those that follow public affairs have higher PSM, likely reflecting several aspects of the concept such as commitment to the public interest.

Along with increasing polarization, the Republican party has become more extreme. The gap between voter preferences and the GOP establishment priorities has widened, and the Republican party is changing the landscape of American politics (see Skopol & Hertel-Fernandez, 2016). Conservative ideologies have long sought to minimize the role of government but are now cutting and reforming programs, government employees, and services at the cost of social equity (e.g., Pynes & Rissler, 2017), ethics (e.g., Santis & Zavattaro, 2019), and public administration (e.g., Goodsell, 2019). Despite the role of political ideology and party in shaping PSM, the concept of PSM influences public preferences, priorities, and behaviors even with political controls.

5.2 PSM and Public Opinion

Given PSM shapes individual behaviors and that high-PSM individuals tend to sort into public sector careers (e.g., Clerkin & Coggburn, 2012; Holt, 2018; Piatak, 2016a; Stritch & Christensen, 2016; Vandenabeele, 2008b; Wright, Hassan, & Christensen, 2017), PSM could play a role in policy making through public opinion, the decision-making of leaders, and bureaucratic discretion. Therefore, we ask how might PSM influence policy preferences and priorities? In addition, since high-PSM individuals tend to exhibit prosocial behaviors outside the workplace, like volunteering (e.g., Christensen et al., 2015; Clerkin & Fotheringham, 2017; Piatak, 2016a; Piatak & Holt, 2020b; Walton et al., 2017), we examine whether the influence of PSM extends to political participation and engagement, such as deciding to run for office, working for a campaign, and attending public meetings. Despite the link between PSM and political ideology and party, PSM significantly influences a wide range of policy preferences even after taking demographic, socioeconomic, and other motivating values like political views into account. Here, we describe our findings in Section 4 on how PSM corresponds to public policy preferences, budget priorities, and political behaviors.

Concern for the commons. We find PSM corresponds to support for all four environmental protection policies examined from regulating carbon emissions and establishing a renewable energy minimum to increased fuel efficiency standards and Clean Air and Water Act enforcement. The environment is a common resource where individual decisions and sacrifices help to ensure sustainability (Ostrom, 1990). Support for environmental protection policies signifies PSM-driven individuals care about the commons. This is in line with experimental studies that find PSM influences contributions in public goods games, especially when others contribute (Esteve et al., 2016), and collaboration in the prisoner's dilemma game (Esteve, van Witteloostuijn, & Boyne, 2015). PSM encompasses a concern for the public interest and self-sacrifice, which likely influences support for environmental protection policies.

Preference for direct government regulation. We find PSM influences a preference for more direct government policies, like regulations. The preference for direct government interventions was found for gun control policies, where PSM corresponded with support for universal background checks and a ban on assault rifles, but opposition to making concealed carry permits easier to obtain. Examining food safety where risk is high and boundaries are blurred, Maestas et al. (2020) find public preferences for uniform regulation at the federal level. Gun control and the environment may be similar types of issues in terms of risk and boundaries, where higher levels of PSM correspond to greater support for regulation. This aligns with Song et al. (2017), who find that bureaucrats with high levels of PSM prefer more direct policy instruments. Perhaps PSM drives a preference for direct policy instruments both on the job and in public opinion.

Domestic focused. We find PSM corresponds to more domestic-oriented policies. For example, Congressional items dealing with international affairs, such as TPP and Iran sanctions, corresponded with lower average PSM. President Trump ran on a campaign of "America first," but for high-PSM individuals, concern for the domestic public remains after controlling for political ideology and political party. Higher levels of PSM correspond with support for education reform, the Highway and Transportation Funding Act, the Medicare Reform Act, and increasing the minimum wage and opposition to repealing the Affordable Care Act. PSM-driven individuals support government institutions enhancing services and aid to the public.

In terms of public opinion on immigration, we find PSM positively influences support for the legal status of immigrants for both workers and children and that PSM drives opposition to deporting illegal immigrants. However, PSM had little relation to more internationally focused policies like increasing visas or banning Muslims or Syrian refugees. PSM includes a concern for the public, perhaps the support for legal status and opposition to deportation reflects this concern for those in the community. Externally focused policies to ban or admit others into the US concern those who are not yet members of the public. PSM corresponds to granting legal rights and protections to current community members.

Protect individual rights. In examining family issues, we find PSM significantly influences support for the protection of individual rights. Higher levels of PSM correspond with opposition to allow employers to decline coverage of abortions in insurance plans and to prohibit the expenditure of funds authorized or appropriated by federal law for any abortion. Since *Roe v. Wade* (1973), freedom to choose to have an abortion without undue burden is a constitutionally protected right. PSM includes elements of compassion, commitment to the public interest, and social justice that support the resolve to uphold constitutional rights. While religion and politics significantly influence normative questions of what should be a constitutionally protected right, such as same-sex marriage and abortion, PSM drives opposition to policies that infringe on constitutionally protected rights.

PSM encompasses normative values like a sense of duty to government, to advance social equity, and to serve the public interest. The values of individual rights and equity stem from the legal approach to public administration with origins in administrative law, judicialization, and constitutional law (Rosenbloom,1983). Scholars have called for a return to democratic and normative values to guide administrative decision-making (e.g., Friedrich, 1940; Mosher, 1982; Roberts, 2019a; Young, Wiley, & Searing, 2020), perhaps PSM captures this common value system.

Focus on accountability. In examining a range of criminal justice policies, we find PSM only corresponds to support for police to wear body cameras. While PSM significantly influences calls for accountability through the administrative policy of requiring police to wear body cameras, PSM was not significantly related to sentencing guidelines nor increasing the number of police officers. Police body-worn cameras (BWCs) have been the subject of great debate.

However, BWCs improve accountability. Qualitative work has found BWCs may improve officer conduct and enhance police legitimacy (Wright II & Headley, 2020), and field experiments found evidence of greater community activity and less intrusive methods, more citations, and fewer arrests (Headley, Guerette, & Shariati, 2017). In addition, a quasi-randomized controlled trial in traffic stops finds BWCs improve citizens' perceptions of police behavior and quality of treatment (Demir, 2019). Although most criminal justice reforms are more a matter of politics, higher levels of PSM correspond to support for BWCs, an administrative policy to enhance the transparency of police discretion. Romzek (2015) cautions: "'Uneven practice' is about the failures to use existing account-ability arrangements to hold individuals and organizations answerable. Sometimes we impose accountability effectively. Often, we do not do it well" (4).

Support for a larger role of government. Perhaps PSM-driven individuals are not concerned with budget policies but rather budget outcomes. Like Moynihan (2013), we find PSM unrelated to public preferences about how to address the federal budget deficit. However, we find across all state budget areas – welfare, health care, education, law enforcement, and transit/infrastructure, PSM corresponds to a preference for increased spending. Perhaps this reflects the understanding of the role of government institutions in society and a preference for government to take a more proactive role to advance the public interest and social equity.

Political participation in government institutions over politics. In examining a range of political behaviors, individuals with higher levels of PSM are more likely to attend local public meetings and consider running for elected office. In this sense, PSM is more related to political activities that serve government institutions, attending public meetings and serving in public positions, rather than politics, such as working for or donating to campaigns. PSM scholars have called for greater attention to elected officials (e.g., Ritz, Brewer, & Neumann, 2016), but results have been mixed. In samples of current elected officials, Ritz (2015) finds certain PSM dimensions correspond to intent to seek re-election, while others find PSM unrelated to re-election intention (Pendersen, Andersen, & Thomsen, 2020). Our findings suggest PSM-driven individuals are more likely to engage with local government institutions through public meeting attendance and even consideration for serving in an elected position. The public service aspect of PSM extends to engaging and serving in local government, but not the realm of politics.

5.3 Limitations and Future Directions

Like any study, our work is not without its limitations. We contribute to research on the antecedents of PSM by examining a broader US sample than a survey of government employees that limits the questions available and biases the antecedents toward those driven to work in the public sphere. Our use of the CCES brings numerous benefits, including the ability to examine a wider range of individual characteristics and beliefs, such as racial categories, sexuality, religion, and political views. However, we are limited to the sub-sample of the CCES to examine the antecedents of PSM and the influence of PSM on attitudes to a range of policy issues. This means some groups of individuals are too small to have precise estimates and need further examination. In addition, we provide a cross-sectional and largely descriptive analysis of how PSM varies across groups and how PSM shapes public opinions and political behaviors. Here, we discuss our suggestions for future research both to overcome data limitations as well as to test causal mechanisms to advance our understanding of PSM.

More inclusive data. To be a more just and inclusive society, we need to learn more about and include data on *all* individuals. We attempt to do so by examining PSM across racial groups and LGBTQ. We, as a field, should move beyond binary questions and examinations of gender. This may require collaborative efforts across scholars and institutions to gather larger data samples to ensure a diverse sample. Asking inclusive survey questions about gender to then exclude non-binary responses because of too few cases is not truly inclusive, nor does it advance our understanding. For example, we find similarities between cis women and transgender males that suggest a biological mechanism underpins the predisposition of women to have higher levels of PSM than men.

Additionally, important cultural differences across race and ethnicity get lost in aggregate binary white/nonwhite comparisons. We find average PSM varies across racial groups, but these differences likely disappear in the aggregate and samples are too small for precise estimates. However, Native Americans have higher average levels of PSM. Research should strive to be representative of all of society. Particularly in public administration, a field centered on public institutions that play a vital role in social equity (e.g., Frederickson, 2015; Gooden, 2015), we need to do better. We need complete data to offer the appropriate prescriptions to government and nonprofit leaders, whether through collaborative surveys, like the CCES (for a discussion of the origins of the survey and benefits of a collaborative survey, see Ansolabehere & Rivers, 2013), or more qualitative work to develop an understanding of racially underrepresented voices.

Acknowledge the role of politics. We live in a political world, for better or worse, and need to acknowledge and account for increasing political polarization. Given much work on PSM and in the field of public administration focuses on the administrative bureaucracy rather than the political realm, sociocultural factors like religion and politics are often excluded. However, religion and politics are intertwined, and politics is playing an ever-increasing role in shaping public opinions, attitudes, and behaviors. For example, we are living in the COVID-19 global pandemic as we write and in the United States, the act of wearing a mask to protect public health is a partisan issue. The politicization of even non-intrusive safety precautions in the midst of a dangerous and life-threatening global disease outbreak underscores the propensity for any government action to become subject to political competition. To advance our field and public management, we need to develop an understanding of the role of politics and how to navigate political dynamics.

We find a link between political ideology and PSM that may animate identity influences. Both the Black-white gap and education gap in PSM shrink after controlling for political ideology and political party. Political views may be a moderator for PSM. For example, political party affiliation moderates the influence of education on environmental views, as more educated Democrats believe in climate change, while more educated Republicans deny climate change (Dunlap et al., 2016). The potential moderating effect of political ideology on PSM and in other areas of public and nonprofit management should be examined.

Testing underlying mechanisms. We contribute to research on the antecedents of PSM by examining additional factors and a broader population, but are limited to the cross-sectional nature of our data. Our findings point to several potential underlying mechanisms to explain why social factors shape PSM that should be tested in future research. As an interdisciplinary field, we often borrow theories from other fields and disciplines, but there is renewed attention to incorporate psychological perspectives (e.g., Grimmelikhuijsen et al., 2017; James et al., 2020). We offer several theories for testing in PSM research and more broadly in public and nonprofit management.

First, we find widows and widowers have higher levels of PSM compared to other marital groups. While this could be for several reasons, such as (re) attachment to kin, new bridging ties through support groups, or greater community connections. We offer socioemotional selectivity theory (Carstensen, 1992), the idea that people seek more meaningful tasks to spend their time, for future testing. People who experience loss may take the perspective that life is short and look for meaningful public service or see the world in a different light.

Second, we find having children increases PSM. Here too, there are several potential mechanisms such as additional social ties, role modeling, or wanting to make the world a better place for future generations. Both to explain the link between having children and PSM as well as to advance our understanding of government and nonprofit employee behaviors, we could use a deeper understanding of how sociological and psychological theories operate in the public sphere. For example, does Erickson's (1963) theory of generativity or Bandura's (1971) social learning theory or Granovetter's (1973) weak ties explain why having children increases PSM? Understanding the underlying mechanism could help public managers and organizations foster PSM.

Law, democratic values, and social justice. PSM predicts public policy preferences and views on the role of government even with controls for a battery of demographic, socioeconomic, and sociocultural factors including political ideology and party identification. We find PSM predicts preferences to preserve common resources, protect individual rights, and support administrative policies to enhance accountability. PSM relates to more domestic policies and more direct policy instruments like government regulations. We also find higher levels of PSM correspond to support for a greater role of government across policy areas in terms of state government funding priorities. Across policy issues, PSM plays some role in shaping public opinion that may relate but is distinct from political views. We suspect this is the confidence and value high-PSM individuals place in public institutions.

With increasing polarization in the United States, and across the globe, we need a unifying value and perspective. Scholars have long called for democratic norms and values to guide bureaucratic decision-making (e.g., Friedrich, 1940; Mosher, 1982) and issues with the politics-administration dichotomy, including the inability to remove politics from administration as well as calls to return to the role of law, have been reignited (e.g., Newbold, 2014; Roberts, 2019a; Young, Wiley, & Searing, 2020). Each lens – political, managerial, and legal – comes with its own normative values and priorities (Rosenbloom, 1983). We need a broader and critical perspective to acknowledge the dark history of public administration (e.g., Roberts, 2019b) and the role of government in institutionalizing racism in the United States (e.g., Alexander & Stivers, 2020; Gooden, 2015). We offer PSM as a broader set of values.

We suggest PSM could play a role in policy making by shaping public opinion that in turn factors into the policy-making process or through policy making of leaders or through bureaucratic discretion. Since we find PSM does indeed shape public policy preferences and individual attitudes, future research should examine how this influences policy making and decision-making in practice. For example, do high-PSM individuals prioritize equity over efficiency? PSM might provide a proxy for a normative perspective that embraces democratic values, acknowledges the role of government, and strives for social justice.

PSM beyond public management. We find higher levels of PSM correspond to attending public meetings and considering running for public office. Perhaps

PSM could be a useful measure for political science and in examinations of political behaviors and participation that center on government institutions. Future research should examine PSM in conjunction with political interest and political knowledge to examine political ambition and political behaviors. Perhaps the incorporation of PSM could overcome the resource-based concerns with many examinations of decisions to run for office (e.g., Holman & Schneider, 2018) that could help not only diversify representation in political positions but also enhance those with PSM values.

6 Conclusion

Public service motivation (PSM) arose to explain differences between the public and private sectors (e.g., Perry & Rainey, 1988; Rainey, 1982; Rainey, Backoff, & Levine, 1976) and predict why people choose to enter public service (Perry & Wise, 1990). PSM has grown to examine much more from employee attitudes and behaviors, like job satisfaction (for a review, see Homberg et al., 2015), performance (e.g., Andersen et al., 2014; Bellé, 2013), and organizational citizenship behavior (e.g., Boyd et al., 2018; Piatak & Holt, 2020a), to prosocial behaviors outside of the workplace, such as volunteering (e.g., Piatak & Holt, 2020b). Given the potential benefits of PSM, we first ask: Who has PSM? More specifically, what demographic, socioeconomic, and sociocultural factors shape PSM? Second, if certain people are more likely to have PSM than others, how does PSM shape public policy preferences and attitudes and does PSM influence political behaviors? PSM may influence policy making from the role of public opinion in the policy process (e.g., Baumgartner & Jones, 2010; Kingdon, 1995; Sabatier & Weible, 2007; Stone, 1988) to the discretion and decision-making of public leaders and bureaucrats (e.g., Lipsky, 2010; Pandey et al., 2016; Stazyk, Davis & Portillo, 2017). Decisions are not politically neutral. As such, scholars have called for normative values to underpin administrative decision-making (e.g., Friedrich, 1940; Mosher, 1982; Roberts, 2019a; Young, Wiley, & Searing, 2020). PSM may provide a common set of normative values to guide policy making and decision-making. We define PSM as the drive to help others, grounded in public institutions.

In examining the antecedents of PSM, several of our findings have implications for PSM research and public management practice. We summarize the lessons from our findings presented in Section 3 and discussed in Section 5 in Table 3. First, PSM is a predisposition. While PSM may be enhanced or inhibited, it is in part a predisposition, as we find evidence for gender to have a genetic influence on levels of PSM. Second, PSM is subject to cultural influences. Just as research finds PSM varies by country context (e.g., Parola et al., 2019), we find PSM varies across racial groups likely due to cultural

Table 3 Lessons learned from the antecedents of PSM

1	PSM is a predisposition.
2	PSM is subject to cultural influences.
3	Social ties matter rather than resources.
4	PSM is shaped by life experiences.
5	PSM is influenced by but distinct from religion and politics.

Table 4 How PSM shapes public opinion

1	Concern for the commons
2	Preference for direct government regulation
3	Domestic focused
4	Protection of individual rights
5	Focus on accountability
6	Support for government institutions over politics

differences. Third, social ties seem to matter more than resources. We find having children and losing a spouse influences PSM with no relation to employment status or income. Fourth, PSM is shaped by life experiences. Both losing a spouse and having children are major life experiences as well as a means to enhance social ties and community connections. Lastly, while religiosity, religion, political views, and political affiliation correspond to levels of PSM, PSM has a distinct influence on policy preferences. Public and nonprofit managers should get to know their employees, citizens, and clients, as whole people.

We find PSM plays a prominent role in shaping public policy preferences. With a foundation in concern for the public, PSM has a distinct influence on public preferences and priorities from demographic, socioeconomic, and political factors. The lessons from the findings presented in Section 4 and discussed in Section 5 are presented in Table 4. First, PSM corresponds with concern for the commons. We find individuals with high PSM support a wide range of environmental policies illustrating a desire to protect common resources. Second, PSM driven individuals prefer direct government regulation. High-PSM individuals prefer more direct government intervention to protect the public interest, which we found across policy areas like environmental protection and gun control. Third, PSM seems domestic-focused. We find PSM has a stronger relation to domestic rather than international policies. In addition, PSM corresponds to protecting immigrants currently in the United States with no relation to policies on those entering the US. Fourth, PSM drives the protection of individual rights. We find high levels of PSM correspond to a preference for policies that prohibit the infringement of constitutionally protected rights. Fifth, PSM corresponds to support for administrative policies that enhance accountability. We find higher levels of PSM correspond to support for administrative policies for greater police transparency, but it is left to effective practice to hold officers accountable. Lastly, PSM corresponds to government support. We find high-PSM individuals support state government spending on a range of public programs. In addition, high-PSM individuals are more likely to consider running for office or to attend local public meetings but do not get involved in political campaigns. In this sense, PSM seems to provide a normative set of values that drives public policy preferences and priorities.

We, both as a field and as a society, should acknowledge the role of politics and strive for justice. We could use a return to (Newbold, 2014; Rosenbloom, 1983) and reanalysis of (e.g., Alexander & Stivers, 2020; Gooden, 2015; Roberts, 2019b) the foundation of our field and democracy. Beyond politics, PSM plays a role in shaping public policy preferences, priorities, and behaviors. PSM may be a useful measure, and perhaps more inclusive measure, for political science in examining political ambition and decisions to run for office. More importantly, PSM provides a measure of normative values that shape public opinion. Scholars have called for democratic values to play a more prominent role in administrative decision-making (e.g., Friedrich, 1940; Mosher, 1982; Roberts, 2019a; Young, Wiley, & Searing, 2020), PSM may provide a useful framework. While there is no quick and easy way to overcome years of polarization, PSM driven individuals seem to hope to do so in the interest of the public good.

References

AbouAssi, K., McGinnis Johnson, J., & Holt, S. B. (2019). Job mobility among millennials: Do they stay or do they go? *Review of Public Personnel Administration, 0734371X19874396.*

Adams, I., & Mastracci, S. (2019). Police body-worn cameras: Development of the perceived intensity of monitoring scale. *Criminal Justice Review, 44*(3), 386–405.

Alexander, J., & Stivers, C. (2020). Racial bias: A buried cornerstone of the administrative state. *Administration & Society, 0095399720921508.*

Allison, G. T. (1980). Public and private management: Are they fundamentally alike in all unimportant respects? In G. M. Shafrtitz & A. C. Hyde (1992), *Classics of Public Administration* (457–474). Belmont, CA: Wordsworth.

Alonso, P., & Lewis, G. B. (2001). Public service motivation and job performance: Evidence from the federal sector. *The American Review of Public Administration, 31*(4), 363–380.

Andersen, L. B. (2009). What determines the behaviour and performance of health professionals? Public service motivation, professional norms and/or economic incentives. *International Review of Administrative Sciences, 75*(1), 79–97.

Andersen, L. B., Heinesen, E., & Pedersen, L. H. (2014). How does public service motivation among teachers affect student performance in schools? *Journal of Public Administration Research and Theory, 24*(3), 651–671.

Andersen, L. B., & Kjeldsen, A. M. (2013). Public service motivation, user orientation, and job satisfaction: A question of employment sector? *International Public Management Journal, 16*(2), 252–274.

Andersen, L. B., Pallesen, T., & Holm Pedersen, L. (2011). Does ownership matter? Public service motivation among physiotherapists in the private and public sectors in Denmark. *Review of Public Personnel Administration, 31*(1), 10–27.

Ansolabehere, S., & Hersh, E. (2012). Validation: What big data reveal about survey misreporting and the real electorate. *Political Analysis, 20*(4), 437–459.

Ansolabehere, S., & Rivers, D. (2013). Cooperative survey research. *Annual Review of Political Science, 16*, 307–329.

Ansolabehere, S., & Schaffner, B. F. (2014). Does survey mode still matter? Findings from a 2010 multi-mode comparison. *Political Analysis, 22*(3), 285–303.

Ansolabehere, S., & Schaffner, B. F. (2017). CCES Common Content, 2016. *Harvard Dataverse.* https://dataverse.harvard.edu/dataset.xhtml?persistentId=doi%3A10.7910/DVN/GDF6Z0.

Asseburg, J., Hattke, J., Hensel, D., Homberg, F., & Vogel, R. (2020). The tacit dimension of public sector attraction in multi-incentive settings. *Journal of Public Administration Research and Theory, 30*(1), 41–59.

Asseburg, J., & Homberg, F. (2020). Public service motivation or sector rewards? Two studies on the determinants of sector attraction. *Review of Public Personnel Administration, 40*(1), 82–111.

Ballart, X., & Rico, G. (2018). Public or nonprofit? Career preferences and dimensions of public service motivation. *Public Administration, 96*(2), 404–420.

Banda, K. K., & Kirkland, J. H. (2018). Legislative party polarization and trust in state legislatures. *American Politics Research, 46*(4), 596–628.

Bandura, A. (1971). *Social Learning Theory.* Morristown, NJ: Prentice Hall.

Baumgartner, F. R., & Jones, B. D. (2010). *Agendas and Instability in American Politics.* Chicago: University of Chicago Press.

Behn, R. D. (1995). The big questions of public management. *Public Administration Review, 55*(4), 313–324.

Bellé, N. (2013). Experimental evidence on the relationship between public service motivation and job performance. *Public Administration Review, 73*(1), 143–153.

Ben-Asher, S., & Bokek-Cohen, Y. A. (2020). Commemoration labor as emotional labor: The emotional costs of being an Israeli militarized national widow. *Gender, Place & Culture,* 1–21.

Borry, E. L., & Henderson, A. C. (2020). Patients, protocols, and prosocial behavior: Rule breaking in Frontline Health Care. *American Review of Public Administration, 50*(1), 45–61.

Boyd, N., Nowell, B., Yang, Z., & Hano, M. C. (2018). Sense of community, sense of community responsibility, and public service motivation as predictors of employee well-being and engagement in public service organizations. *American Review of Public Administration, 48*(5), 428–443.

Boyne, G. A. (2002). Public and private management: What's the difference? *Journal of Management Studies, 39*(1), 97–122.

Bozeman, B., & Ponomariov, B. (2009). Sector switching from a business to a government job: Fast-track career or fast track to nowhere? *Public Administration Review, 69*(1), 77–91.

Bozeman, B., & Su, X. (2015). Public service motivation concepts and theory: A critique. *Public Administration Review, 75*(5), 700–710.

Brewer, G. A. (2003). Building social capital: Civic attitudes and behavior of public servants. *Journal of Public Administration Research and Theory, 13*(1), 5–26.

Brewer, G. A., Ritz, A., & Vandenabeele, W. (2012). Introduction to a symposium on public service motivation: An international sampling of research. *International Journal of Public Administration, 35*: 1–4.

Brewer, G. A., & Selden, S. C. (1998). Whistle blowers in the federal civil service: New evidence of the public service ethic. *Journal of Public Administration Research and Theory, 8*(3), 413–440.

Bright, L. (2005). Public employees with high levels of public service motivation: Who are they, where are they, and what do they want? *Review of Public Personnel Administration, 25*(2), 138–154.

Bright, L. (2008). Does public service motivation really make a difference on the job satisfaction and turnover intentions of public employees? *American Review of Public Administration, 38*(2), 149–166.

Bright, L. (2011). Does public service motivation affect the occupation choices of public employees?. *Public Personnel Management, 40*(1), 11–24.

Camilleri, E. (2007). Antecedents affecting public service motivation. *Personnel Review, 36*(3), 356–377.

Camilleri, E., & Van Der Heijden, B. I. (2007). Organizational commitment, public service motivation, and performance within the public sector. *Public Performance & Management Review, 31*(2), 241–274.

Campbell, J. W., & Im, T. (2016). PSM and turnover intention in public organizations: Does change-oriented organizational citizenship behavior play a role? *Review of Public Personnel Administration, 36*(4), 323–346.

Carr, D., & Utz, R. L. (2020). Families in later life: A decade in review. *Journal of Marriage and Family, 82*(1), 346–363.

Carstensen, L. L. (1992). Social and emotional patterns in adulthood: Support for socioemotional selectivity theory. *Psychology and Aging, 7*(3), 331–338.

Charbonneau, É., & Van Ryzin, G. G. (2017). Exploring the deep antecedent of public service motivation. *International Journal of Public Administration, 40*(5), 401–407.

Chetkovich, C. (2003). What's in a sector? The shifting career plans of public policy students. *Public Administration Review, 63*(6), 660–674.

Christensen, R. K., Moon, K. K., & Whitford, A. B. (2020). Genetics and sector of employment. *International Public Management Journal*, 1–11.

Christensen, R. K., Paarlberg, L., & Perry, J. L. (2017). Public service motivation research: Lessons for practice. *Public Administration Review, 77*(4), 529–542.

Christensen, R. K., Stritch, J. M., Kellough, J. E., & Brewer, G. A. (2015). Identifying student traits and motives to service-learn: Public service orientation among new college freshmen. *Journal of Higher Education Outreach and Engagement, 19*(4), 39–62.

Christensen, R. K., & Wright, B. E. (2011). The effects of public service motivation on job choice decisions: Disentangling the contributions of person-organization fit and person-job fit. *Journal of Public Administration Research and Theory, 21*(4), 723–743.

Clerkin, R. M., & Coggburn, J. D. (2012). The dimensions of public service motivation and sector work preferences. *Review of Public Personnel Administration, 32*(3), 209–235.

Clerkin, R. M., & Fotheringham, E. (2017). Exploring the relationship between public service motivation and formal and informal volunteering. *Journal of Public and Nonprofit Affairs, 3*(1), 23–39.

Clerkin, R. M., Paynter, S. R., & Taylor, J. K. (2009). Public service motivation in undergraduate giving and: Volunteering decisions. *American Review of Public Administration, 39*(6), 675–698.

Cole, R. L., & Kincaid, J. (2000). Public opinion and American federalism: Perspectives on taxes, spending, and trust – An ACIR update. *Publius: The Journal of Federalism, 30*(1), 189–201.

Coleman, J.S. (1988). Social capital in the creation of human capital. *American Journal of Sociology, 94*(suppl.): S95–S120.

Corporation for National and Community Service. (2009). First Lady Michelle Obama Issues Call to Service to Nation's Volunteer Leaders. www.national service.gov/newsroom/press-releases/ 2009/first-lady-michelle-obama-issues-call-service-nation%E2%80%99s-volunteer.

Coursey, D. H., & Pandey, S. K. (2007). Public service motivation measurement: Testing an abridged version of Perry's proposed scale. *Administration & Society, 39*(5), 547–568.

Dancey, L., & Sheagley, G. (2013). Heuristics behaving badly: Party cues and voter knowledge. *American Journal of Political Science, 57*(2), 312–325.

Davis, R. S., Stazyk, E. C., & Klingeman, C. M. (2020). Accounting for personal disposition and organizational context: connecting role ambiguity, public service motivation, and whistle-blowing in federal agencies. *International Journal of Human Resource Management, 31*(10), 1313–1332.

de Tocqueville, A. (1831, 2002). *Democracy in America*. Washington, DC: Regnery Publishing.

DeHart-Davis, L., Marlowe, J., & Pandey, S. K. (2006). Gender dimensions of public service motivation. *Public Administration Review, 66*(6), 873–887.

Demir, M. (2019). Citizens' perceptions of body-worn cameras (BWCs): Findings from a quasi-randomized controlled trial. *Journal of Criminal Justice, 60*, 130–139.

Doherty, C. (2014). *Political Polarization in the American Public: How Increasing Ideological Uniformity and Partisan Antipathy Affect Politics, Compromise and Everyday Life.* Washington, DC: Pew Research Center.

Dolan, K., & Hansen, M. A. (2020). The Variable Nature of the Gender Gap in Political Knowledge. *Journal of Women, Politics & Policy, 41*(2), 127–143.

Downs, A. (1972). Up and down with ecology: The issue-attention cycle. *Public Interest, 28*: 38–50.

Dunlap, R. E., McCright, A. M., & Yarosh, J. H. (2016). The political divide on climate change: Partisan polarization widens in the US. *Environment: Science and Policy for Sustainable Development, 58*(5), 4–23.

Elchardus, M., & Spruyt, B. (2009). The culture of academic disciplines and the sociopolitical attitudes of students: A test of selection and socialization effects. *Social Science Quarterly, 90*(2): 446–460.

Erikson, E. (1963). *Childhood and Society.* 2nd ed. New York: W. W. Norton.

Esteve, M., Urbig, D., Van Witteloostuijn, A., & Boyne, G. (2016). Prosocial behavior and public service motivation. *Public Administration Review, 76*(1), 177–187.

Esteve, M., Van Witteloostuijn, A., & Boyne, G. (2015). The effects of public service motivation on collaborative behavior: Evidence from three experimental games. *International Public Management Journal, 18*(2), 171–189.

Frederickson, H. G. (1997). *The Spirit of Public Administration.* San Francisco: Jossey-Bass.

Frederickson, H. G. (2015). *Social Equity and Public Administration: Origins, Developments, and Applications: Origins, Developments, and Applications.* London: Routledge.

Friedrich, C. J. (1940). Public policy and the nature of administrative responsibility. In C. J. Friedrich and E. S. Mason (eds.), *Public Policy* (3–24). Cambridge, MA: Harvard University Press.

Gaynor, T. S., & Wilson, M. E. (2020). Social vulnerability and equity: The disproportionate impact of COVID-19. *Public Administration Review, 80*(5), 832-838.

Georgellis, Y., Iossa, E., & Tabvuma, V. (2011). Crowding out intrinsic motivation in the public sector. *Journal of Public Administration Research and Theory, 21*(3), 473–493.

Gerring, J. (1999). What makes a concept good? A criterial framework for understanding concept formation in the social sciences. *Polity, 31*(3), 357–393.

Goelzhauser, G., & Konisky, D. M. (2020). The State of American Federalism 2019–2020: Polarized and Punitive Intergovernmental Relations. Publius. *Journal of Federalism.* https://doi.org/10.1093/publius/pjaa021.

Gooden, S. T. (2015). *Race and Social Equity: A Nervous Area of Government*. London: Routledge.

Goodsell, C. T. (2019). The anti-public administration presidency: The damage Trump has wrought. *American Review of Public Administration, 49*(8), 871–883.

Gould-Williams, J. S., Mostafa, A. M. S., & Bottomley, P. (2015). Public service motivation and employee outcomes in the Egyptian public sector: Testing the mediating effect of person-organization fit. *Journal of Public Administration Research and Theory, 25*(2), 597–622.

Granovetter, M. S. (1973). The strength of weak ties. *American Journal of Sociology, 78,* 1360–1380.

Grimmelikhuijsen, S., Jilke, S., Olsen, A. L., & Tummers, L. (2017). Behavioral public administration: Combining insights from public administration and psychology. *Public Administration Review, 77*(1), 45–56.

Gross, H. P., Thaler, J., & Winter, V. (2019). Integrating public service motivation in the job-demands-resources model: An empirical analysis to explain employees' performance, absenteeism, and presenteeism. *International Public Management Journal, 22*(1), 176–206.

Hall, J. L., Zavattaro, S. M., Battaglio, R. P., & Hail, M. W. (2020). Global reflection, conceptual exploration, and evidentiary assimilation: COVID-19 viewpoint symposium introduction. *Public Administration Review, 80*(4), 590–594.

Harari, M. B., Herst, D. E., Parola, H. R., & Carmona, B. P. (2017). Organizational correlates of public service motivation: A meta-analysis of two decades of empirical research. *Journal of Public Administration Research and Theory, 27*(1), 68–84.

Harris, A. (2018). America is divided by education. *The Atlantic.*

Hansen, J. R. (2014).From public to private sector: Motives and explanations for sector switching. *Public Management Review, 16*(4), 590–607.

Headley, A. M., Guerette, R. T., & Shariati, A. (2017). A field experiment of the impact of body- worn cameras (BWCs) on police officer behavior and perceptions. *Journal of Criminal Justice, 53,* 102–109.

Hetherington, M. J., Long, M. T., & Rudolph, T. J. (2016). Revisiting the myth: New evidence of a polarized electorate. *Public Opinion Quarterly, 80*(S1), 321–350.

Hetherington, M. J., & Rudolph, T. J. (2015). *Why Washington Won't Work: Polarization, Political Trust, and the Governing Crisis*. Chicago: University of Chicago Press.

Holbein, J. B. (2017). Childhood skill development and adult political participation. *American Political Science Review, 111*(3), 572–583.

Holman, M. R., & Schneider, M. C. (2018). Gender, race, and political ambition: How intersectionality and frames influence interest in political office. *Politics, Groups, and Identities*, *6*(2), 264–280.

Holt, S. B. (2018). For those who care: The effect of public service motivation on sector selection. *Public Administration Review*, *78*(3), 457–471.

Holt, S. B. (2019). The influence of high schools on developing public service motivation. *International Public Management Journal*, *22*(1), 127–175.

Holt, S. B. (2020). Giving time: Examining sector differences in volunteering intensity. *Journal of Public Administration Research and Theory*, *30*(1), 22–40.

Homberg, F., McCarthy, D., & Tabvuma, V. (2015). A meta-analysis of the relationship between public service motivation and job satisfaction. *Public Administration Review*, *75*, 711–722.

Houston, D. J. (2000). Public-service motivation: A multivariate test. *Journal of public Administration Research and Theory*, *10*(4), 713–728.

Houston, D. M. (2019). Polarization and the politics of education: What moves partisan opinion? *Educational Policy*, 0895904818823745.

Houston, D. J., & Cartwright, K. E. (2007). Spirituality and public service. *Public Administration Review*, *67*(1), 88–102.

Huang, W. L., & Feeney, M. K. (2016). Citizen participation in local government decision making: The role of manager motivation. *Review of Public Personnel Administration*, *36*(2), 188–209.

Ingrams, A. (2020). Organizational citizenship behavior in the public and private sectors: A multilevel test of public service motivation and traditional antecedents. *Review of Public Personnel Administration*, *40*(2), 222–244.

Iyengar, S., Sood, G., & Lelkes, Y. (2012). Affect, not ideologya social identity perspective on polarization. *Public Opinion Quarterly*, *76*(3), 405–431.

James, O., Moynihan, D. P., Olsen, A. L. & Van Ryzin, G. G. (2020). *Behavioral Public Performance*. Cambridge: Cambridge University Press.

Jenkins, R. (2014). *Social Identity*. London: Routledge.

Jennings, M. K. (1998). Political trust and the roots of devolution. In V. Braithwaite & M. Levi (eds.), *Trust and Governance* (vol. *1*, 218–244). New York: Russel Sage Foundation.

Jensen, U. T., Andersen, L. B., & Holten, A. L. (2017). Explaining a dark side: Public service motivation, presenteeism, and absenteeism. *Review of Public Personnel Administration*, *39*(4): 487–510.

Jensen, U. T., Andersen, L. B., & Jacobsen, C. B. (2019). Only when we agree! How value congruence moderates the impact of goal-oriented leadership on public service motivation. *Public Administration Review*, *79*(1), 12–24.

Kim, S. (2012). Does person-organization fit matter in the public-sector? Testing the mediating effect of person-organization fit in the relationship between public service motivation and work attitudes. *Public Administration Review, 72*(6), 830–840.

Kim, S. (2017). National culture and public service motivation: Investigating the relationship using Hofstede's five cultural dimensions. *International Review of Administrative Sciences, 83*(suppl.), 23–40.

Kim, S. (2020). Education and Public Service Motivation: A Longitudinal Study of High School Graduates. *Public Administration Review,* 1–13.

Kim, S., Vandenabeele, W., Wright, B. E., Andersen, L. B., Cerase, F. P., Christensen, R. K., . . . & Palidauskaite, J. (2013). Investigating the structure and meaning of public service motivation across populations: Developing an international instrument and addressing issues of measurement invariance. *Journal of Public Administration Research and Theory, 23*(1), 79–102.

Kingdon, J. W. (1995). *Agendas, Alternatives, and Public Policies.* 2nd ed. New York: Harper Collins.

Kjeldsen, A. M. (2014). Dynamics of public service motivation: Attraction, selection and socialization in the production and regulation of social services. *Public Administration Review, 74*(1), 101–112.

Kjeldsen, A. M., & Jacobsen, C. B. (2013). Public service motivation and employment sector: Attraction or socialization? *Journal of Public Administration Research and Theory, 23*(4), 899–926.

Koehler, M., & H. G. Rainey. (2008). Interdisciplinary Foundations of Public Service Motivation. In J. L. Perry & A. Hondeghem (eds.), *Motivation in Public Management: The Call of Public Service* (33–54). New York: Oxford University Press.

Korac, S., Saliterer, I., & Weigand, B. (2019). Factors affecting the preference for public sector employment at the pre-entry level: A systematic review. *International Public Management Journal, 22*(5), 797–840.

Kristof-Brown, A. L., R. D. Zimmerman, & E. C. Johnson. 2005. Consequences of individuals' fit at work: A meta-analysis of person-job, person-organization, person-group, and person-supervisor fit. *Personnel Psychology, 58*(2): 281–342.

Lauderdale, B. E., Hanretty, C., & Vivyan, N. (2018). Decomposing public opinion variation into ideology, idiosyncrasy, and instability. *Journal of Politics, 80*(2), 707–712.

Leland, S., Chattopadhyay, J., Maestas, C., & Piatak, J. (2020). Policy venue preference and relative trust in government in federal systems. *Governance.* https://doi.org/10.1111/gove.12501.

Lewis, G. B., & Frank, S. A. (2002). Who wants to work for the government? *Public Administration Review, 62*(4), 395–404.

Lipsky, M. (2010). *Street-Level Bureaucracy: Dilemmas of the Individual in Public Service.* New York: Russell Sage Foundation.

Maestas, C., Chattopadhyay, J., Leland, S., & Piatak, J. (2020). Fearing food: The influence of risk perceptions on public preferences for uniform and centralized risk regulation. *Policy Studies Journal, 48*(2), 447–468.

Meier, K. J. (2015). Proverbs and the evolution of public administration. *Public Administration Review, 75*(1), 15–24.

Meier, K. J., Stewart, J., & England, R. E. (1989). *Race, Class, and Education: The Politics of Second-Generation Discrimination.* Madison: University of Wisconsin Press.

Mosher, F. C. (1982). *Democracy and the Public Service.* New York: Oxford University Press.

Moynihan, D. P. (2013). Does public service motivation lead to budget maximization? Evidence from an experiment. *International Public Management Journal, 16*(2), 179–196.

Moynihan, D. P., & Pandey, S. K. (2007). The role of organizations in fostering public service motivation. *Public Administration Review, 67*(1), 40–53.

Musick, M., & Wilson, J. (2008). *Volunteers: A Social Profile.* Indianapolis: Indiana University Press.

Naff, K. C., & Crum, J. (1999). Working for America: Does public service motivation make a difference? *Review of Public Personnel Administration, 19*(4), 5–16.

Nelson, A., & Piatak, J. (2019). Intersectionality, leadership, and inclusion: How do racially underrepresented women fare in the federal government? *Review of Public Personnel Administration,* 1–25.

Newbold, S. P. (2014). Why a constitutional approach matters for advancing new democratic governance. In D. Morgan & B. Cook (eds.), *New Public Governance: A Regime-Centered Perspective* (13–22). London: Routledge.

Nowell, B., Izod, A. M., Ngaruiya, K. M., & Boyd, N. M. (2016). Public service motivation and sense of community responsibility: Comparing two motivational constructs in understanding leadership within community collaboratives. *Journal of Public Administration Research and Theory, 26*(4), 663–676.

Oelberger, C. R. (2019). The dark side of deeply meaningful work: Work-relationship turmoil and the moderating role of occupational value homophily. *Journal of Management Studies, 56*(3), 558–588.

O'Leary, C. (2019). Public service motivation: A rationalist critique. *Public Personnel Management, 48*(1), 82–96.

Ostrom, E. (1990). *Governing the Commons: The Evolution of Institutions for Collective Action.* Cambridge: Cambridge University Press.

Pacheco, J. (2012). The social contagion model: Exploring the role of public opinion on the diffusion of antismoking legislation across the American states. *Journal of Politics, 74*(1), 187–202.

Pandey, S. K., Davis, R. S., Pandey, S., & Peng, S. (2016). Transformational leadership and the use of normative public values: Can employees be inspired to serve larger purposes? *Public Administration, 94*, 204–222.

Pandey, S. K., & Stazyk, E. C. (2008). Antecedents and correlates of public service motivation. In J. L. Perry & A. Hondeghem (eds.), *Motivation in Public Management: The Call of Public Service* (101–117). New York: Oxford University Press.

Pandey, S. K., Wright, B. E., & Moynihan, D. P. (2008). Public service motivation and interpersonal citizenship behavior in public organizations: Testing a preliminary model. *International Public Management Journal, 11*(1), 89–108.

Parker, K. (2019). The growing partisan divide in views of higher education. *PEW Research Center: Social and Demographic Trends, 1–7.*

Parola, H. R., Harari, M. B., Herst, D. E., & Prysmakova, P. (2019). Demographic determinants of public service motivation: a meta-analysis of PSM-age and-gender relationships. *Public Management Review, 21*(10), 1397–1419.

Pearce, L. D., Hayward, G. M., and Pearlman, J. A. (2017). Measuring five dimensions of religiosity across adolescence. *Review of Religious Research, 59*(3), 367–393.

Pearl, S. (2020). Staying angry: Black women's resistance to racialized forgiveness in US police shootings. *Women's Studies in Communication, 43*(3), 279–291.

Pedersen, L. H. (2014). Committed to the public interest? Motivation and behavioural outcomes among local councillors. *Public Administration, 92*(4), 886–901.

Pedersen, L. H., Andersen, L. B., & Thomsen, N. (2020). Motivated to act and take responsibility–integrating insights from community psychology in PSM research. *Public Management Review, 22*(7), 999–1023.

Pedersen, M. J. (2013). Public service motivation and attraction to public versus private sector employment: Academic field of study as moderator? *International Public Management Journal, 16*, 357–385

Perry, J. L. (1996). Measuring public service motivation: An assessment of construct reliability and validity. *Journal of Public Administration Research and Theory, 6*(1), 5–22.

Perry, J. L. (1997). Antecedents of public service motivation. *Journal of Public Administration Research and Theory, 7*(2), 181–197.

Perry, J. L., Brudney, J. L., Coursey, D., & Littlepage, L. (2008). What drives morally committed citizens? A study of the antecedents of public service motivation. *Public Administration Review, 68*(3), 445–458.

Perry, J. L., & Hondeghem, A. (eds.). 2008. *Motivation in Public Management: The Call of Public Service*. Oxford: Oxford University Press.

Perry, J. L., Hondeghem, A., & Wise, L. R. (2010). Revisiting the motivational bases of public service: Twenty years of research and an agenda for the future. *Public Administration Review, 70*(5), 681–690.

Perry, J. L., & Rainey, H. G. (1988). The public-private distinction in organization theory: A critique and research strategy. *Academy of Management Review, 13*(2), 182–201.

Perry, J. L., & Vandenabeele, W. (2015). Public service motivation research: Achievements, challenges, and future directions. *Public Administration Review, 75*(5), 692–699.

Piatak, J. S. (2015). Altruism by job sector: Can public sector employees lead the way in rebuilding social capital? *Journal of Public Administration Research and Theory, 25*(3): 877–900.

Piatak, J. S. (2016a). Public service motivation, prosocial behaviours, and career ambitions. *International Journal of Manpower, 37*(5): 804–821.

Piatak, J. S. (2016b). Time is on my side: A framework to examine when unemployed individuals volunteer. *Nonprofit and Voluntary Sector Quarterly, 45*(6): 1169–1190.

Piatak, J. S. (2017). Sector switching in good times and in bad: Are public sector employees less likely to change sectors? *Public Personnel Management, 46*(4): 327–341.

Piatak, J. (2019). Weathering the storm: The impact of cutbacks on public employees. *Public Personnel Management, 48*(1): 97–119.

Piatak, J. (forthcoming). Employee motivation across job sectors. In R. S. Davis & E. C. Stazyk (eds.), *The Handbook of Research on Motivation in Public Administration*. Edward Elgar Publishing.

Piatak, J., Dietz, N., & McKeever, B. (2019). Bridging or deepening the digital divide: Influence of household internet access on formal and informal volunteering. *Nonprofit and Voluntary Sector Quarterly, 48*(2S), 123S–150S.

Piatak, J. S., Douglas, J. W., & Raudla, R. (2020). The role perceptions of government professionals: The effects of gender, educational field, and prior job sector. *Public Management Review, 22*(10), 1515–1534.

Piatak, J. S., & Holt, S. B. (2020a). Disentangling altruism and public service motivation: Who exhibits organizational citizenship behaviour? *Public Management Review, 22*(7), 949–973.

Piatak, J. S., & Holt, S. B. (2020b). Prosocial behaviors: A matter of altruism or public Service motivation? *Journal of Public Administration Research and Theory, 30*(3), 504–518.

Piatak, J., Mohr, Z., & McDonald, J. (2020). Rule formalization, gender, and gender congruence: Examining prosocial rule breaking for internal and external stakeholders. *International Public Management Journal.* https://doi.org/10.1080/10967494.2020.1790445.

Piatak, J., Sowa, J., Jacobson, W., & Johnson, J. M. (forthcoming). Infusing public service motivation (PSM) throughout the employment relationship: A review of PSM and the human resource management process. *International Public Management Journal.* https://doi.org/10.1080/10967494.2020.1805381.

Prior, M. (2010). You've either got it or you don't? The stability of political interest over the life cycle. *Journal of Politics, 72,* 747–766.

Putnam, R. D. (2000). *Bowling alone: The collapse and revival of American community.* New York: Simon and Schuster.

Putnam, R. D., & Campbell, D. E. (2012). *American Grace: How Religion Divides and Unites Us.* New York: Simon and Schuster.

Pynes, J. E., & Rissler, G. E. (2017). Social equity in the Trump era: What can local public administrators do to improve social equity for their residents and community in the face of federal cuts? *State and Local Government Review, 49*(1), 48–59.

Rainey, H. G. (1982). Reward preferences among public and private managers: In search of the service ethic. *American Review of Public Administration, 16*(4), 288–302.

Rainey, H. G. (2014). *Understanding and Managing Public Organizations,* 5th edition. New York: John Wiley & Sons.

Rainey, H. G., Backoff, R. W., & Levine, C. H. (1976). Comparing public and private organizations. *Public Administration Review, 36*(2), 233–244.

Rainey, H. G., & Bozeman, B. (2000). Comparing public and private organizations: Empirical research and the power of the a priori. *Journal of Public Administration Research and Theory, 10*(2), 447–470.

Rainey, H. G., & Steinbauer, P. (1999). Galloping elephants: Developing elements of a theory of effective government organizations. *Journal of Public Administration Research and Theory, 9*(1), 1–32.

Riccucci, N. M. (2018). Antecedents of public service motivation: The role of gender. *Perspectives on Public Management and Governance, 1*(2), 115–126.

Ripoll, G. (2019a). In charge of safeguarding the public interest: the role of goal clarity in shaping public service motivation and the acceptance of unethical behaviours. *International Review of Administrative Sciences,* 0020852319878255.

Ripoll, G. (2019b). Disentangling the relationship between public service motivation and ethics: An interdisciplinary approach. *Perspectives on Public Management and Governance, 2*(1), 21–37.

Ripoll, G., & Breaugh, J. (2019). At their wits' end? Economic stress, motivation and unethical judgement of public servants. *Public Management Review, 21*(10), 1516–1537.

Ritz, A. (2015). Public service motivation and politics: Behavioural consequences among local councillors in Switzerland. *Public Administration, 93*(4), 1121–1137.

Ritz, A., Brewer, G. A., & Neumann, O. (2016). Public service motivation: A systematic literature review and outlook. *Public Administration Review, 76*(3), 414–426.

Ritz, A., Giauque, D., Varone, F., & Anderfuhren-Biget, S. (2014). From leadership to citizenship behavior in public organizations: When values matter. *Review of Public Personnel Administration, 34*(2), 128–152.

Roberts, A. (2019a). Shaking hands with Hitler: The politics-administration dichotomy and engagement with fascism. *Public Administration Review, 79*(2), 267–276.

Roberts, A. (2019b). Bearing the white man's burden: American empire and the origin of public administration. *Perspectives on Public Management and Governance, 3*(3), 185–196.

Roberts, A. (2020). The third and fatal shock: How the pandemic killed the millennial paradigm. *Public Administration Review, 80*(4), 603–609.

Romzek, B. S. (2015). Living accountability: Hot rhetoric, cool theory, and uneven practice. *PS, Political Science & Politics, 48*(1), 27.

Rose, R. P. (2013). Preferences for careers in public work: Examining the government–nonprofit divide among undergraduates through public service motivation. *American Review of Public Administration, 43*(4), 416–437.

Rosenbloom, D. H. (1983). Public administrative theory and the separation of powers. *Public Administration Review, 43*(3), 219–227.

Sabatier, P. A., & Weible, C. M. (2007). The advocacy coalition framework. *Theories of the Policy Process, 2,* 189–220.

Sanabria-Pulido, P. (2018). Public service motivation and job sector choice: Evidence from a developing country. *International Journal of Public Administration, 41*(13), 1107–1118.

Santis, E. L., & Zavattaro, S. M. (2019). Performative ethics in the Trump era: A postmodern examination. *Public Integrity, 21*(5), 503–511.

Schneider, B. (1987). The people make the place. *Personnel Psychology, 40*(3), 437–453.

Scott, P. G., & Pandey, S. K. (2005). Red tape and public service motivation: Findings from a national survey of managers in state health and human services agencies. *Review of Public Personnel Administration, 25*(2), 155–180.

Seider, S. C., S. A. Rabinowicz, and S. C. Gillmor. (2011). The impact of philosophy and theology service-learning experiences upon the public service motivation of participating college students. *Journal of Higher Education, 82*(5), 597–628.

Shim, D. C., & Faerman, S. (2017). Government employees' organizational citizenship behavior: The impacts of public service motivation, organizational identification, and subjective OCB norms. *International Public Management Journal, 20*(4), 531–559.

Simas, E. N., Clifford, S., & Kirkland, J. H. (2020). How empathic concern fuels political polarization. *American Political Science Review, 114*(1), 258–269.

Simon, H. A. (2013). *Administrative Behavior.* New York: Simon and Schuster.

Simmons, R. (November 22, 2019). The Harvard case on considering race in admissions is a victory for diversity. *Washington Post.* www.washingtonpost .com/opinions/why-we-need-intentionally-diverse-populations-on-college-campuses/2019/11/22/43aa8dce-0c77-11ea-97ac-a7ccc8dd1ebc_story.html.

Skocpol, T., & Hertel-Fernandez, A. (2016). The Koch network and republican party extremism. *Perspectives on Politics, 14*(3), 681–699.

Song, M., Kwon, I., Cha, S., & Min, N. (2017). The effect of public service motivation and job level on bureaucrats' preferences for direct policy instruments. *Journal of Public Administration Research and Theory, 27*(1), 36–51.

Stazyk, E. C., & Davis, R. S. (2015). Taking the "high road": Does public service motivation alter ethical decision making processes? *Public Administration, 93*(3), 627–645.

Stazyk, E. C., Davis, R. S., & Portillo, S. (2017). More dissimilar than alike? Public values preferences across US minority and white managers. *Public Administration, 95*(3), 605–622.

Steijn, B. (2008). Person-environment fit and public service motivation. *International Public Management Journal, 11*(1), 13–27.

Stone, D. A. (1988). *Policy Paradox and Political Reason.* Glenview, IL: Scott Foresman & Co.

Stritch, J. M., & Christensen, R. K. (2016).Raising the next generation of public servants? Parental influence on volunteering behavior and public service career aspirations. *International Journal of Manpower, 37*(5): 840–858.

Stubager, R. (2008). Education effects on authoritarian–libertarian values: A question of socialization. *British Journal of Sociology, 59*(2), 327–350.

Taylor, J. (2007). The impact of public service motives on work outcomes in Australia: A comparative multi-dimensional analysis. *Public Administration*, *85*(4), 931–959.

Taylor, J. (2008). Organizational influences, public service motivation and work outcomes: An Australian study. *International Public Management Journal*, *11*(1), 67–88.

Taylor, J. (2014). Public service motivation, relational job design, and job satisfaction in local government. *Public Administration*, *92*(4), 902–918.

Thomas, R. M. (ed.). (2016). *Politics and Education: Cases from Eleven Nations*. Amsterdam: Elsevier.

Tschirhart, M., Reed, K. K., Freeman, S. J., & Anker, A. L. (2008). Is the grass greener? Sector shifting and choice of sector by MPA and MBA graduates. *Nonprofit and Voluntary Sector Quarterly*, *37*(4), 668–688.

US Department of Justice. (2020). Justice Department Finds Yale Illegally Discriminates Against Asians and Whites in Undergraduate Admissions in Violation of Federal Civil-Rights Laws, August 13, 2020. www.justice.gov/opa/pr/justice-department-finds-yale-illegally-discriminates-against-asians-and-whites-undergraduate.

Vandenabeele, W. (2007). Toward a theory of public service motivation: An institutional approach. *Public Management Review*, *9*, 545–556.

Vandenabeele, W. (2008a). Development of a public service motivation measurement scale: Corroborating and extending Perry's measurement instrument. *International Public Management Journal*, *11*(1), 143–167.

Vandenabeele, W. (2008b). Government calling: Public service motivation as an element in selecting government as an employer of choice. *Public Administration*, *86*(4), 1089–1105.

Vandenabeele, W. (2009). The mediating effect of job satisfaction and organizational commitment on self-reported performance: more robust evidence of the PSM – performance relationship. *International Review of Administrative Sciences*, *75*(1), 11–34.

Vandenabeele, W. (2011). Who wants to deliver public service? Do institutional antecedents of public service motivation provide an answer? *Review of Public Personnel Administration*, *31*(1), 87–107.

Vandenabeele, W., Brewer, G. A., & Ritz, A. (2014). Past, present, and future of public service motivation research. *Public Administration*, *92*(4), 779–789.

Vandenabeele, W., Ritz, A, & Neumann, O. (2018). Public service motivation: State of the art and conceptual cleanup. In E. Ongaro & S. Van Thiel (eds.), *The Palgrave Handbook of Public Administration and Management in Europe* (261–78). London: Palgrave Macmillan.

Vandenabeele, W., & Van de Walle, S. (2008). International differences in public service motivation: Comparing regions across the world. In J. L. Perry & A. Hondeghem (eds.), *Motivation in Public Management: The Call of Public Service* (101–117). New York: Oxford University Press.

Van der Wal, Z., & Oosterbaan, A. (2013). Government or business? Identifying determinants of MPA and MBA students' career preferences. *Public Personnel Management, 42*(2), 239–258.

Van Loon, N. M., Vandenabeele, W., & Leisink, P. (2017). Clarifying the relationship between public service motivation and in-role and extra-role behaviors: The relative contributions of person-job and person-organization fit. *American Review of Public Administration, 47*(6), 699–713.

Van Witteloostuijn, A., Esteve, M., & Boyne, G. (2017). Public sector motivation ad fonts: Personality traits as antecedents of the motivation to serve the public interest. *Journal of Public Administration Research and Theory, 27*(1), 20–35.

Walton, M. A., Clerkin, R. M., Christensen, R. K., Paarlberg, L. E., Nesbit, R., & Tschirhart, M. (2017). Means, motive and opportunity: Exploring board volunteering. *Personnel Review, 46(1):* 115–135.

Ward, K. D. (2014). Cultivating public service motivation through AmeriCorps service: A longitudinal study. *Public Administration Review, 74*(1), 114–125.

Wright, B. E., Christensen, R. K., & Pandey, S. K. (2013). Measuring public service motivation: Exploring the equivalence of existing global measures. *International Public Management Journal, 16*(2), 197–223.

Wright, B. E., & Grant, A. M. (2010). Unanswered questions about public service motivation: Designing research to address key issues of emergence and effects. *Public Administration Review, 70*(5), 691–700.

Wright, B. E., Hassan, S., & Christensen, R. K. (2017). Job choice and performance: Revisiting core assumptions about public service motivation. *International Public Management Journal, 20*(1), 108–131.

Wright, B. E., Hassan, S., & Park, J. (2016). Does a public service ethic encourage ethical behaviour? Public service motivation, ethical leadership and the willingness to report ethical problems. *Public Administration, 94*(3), 647–663.

Wright, B. E., & Pandey, S. K. (2008). Public service motivation and the assumption of person – Organization fit: Testing the mediating effect of value congruence. *Administration & Society, 40*(5), 502–521.

Wright, B. E., & Pandey, S. K. (2011). Public organizations and mission valence: When does mission matter? *Administration & Society, 43*(1), 22–44.

Wright II, J. E., & Headley, A. M. (2020). Can technology work for policing? Citizen perceptions of police-body worn cameras. *American Review of Public Administration*, 0275074020945632.

Wright II, J. E., & Merritt, C. C. (2020). Social equity and COVID-19: The case of African Americans. *Public Administration Review, 80(5):*820–826.

Young, S. L., Wiley, K. K., & Searing, E. A. (2020). "Squandered in real time": How public management theory underestimated the public administration–politics dichotomy. *American Review of Public Administration*, 0275074020941669.

Zaller, J. R. (1992). *The Nature and Origins of Mass Opinion*. Cambridge: Cambridge University Press.

Cambridge Elements ☰

Public and Nonprofit Administration

Andrew Whitford

University of Georgia

Andrew Whitford is Alexander M. Crenshaw Professor of Public Policy in the School of Public and International Affairs at the University of Georgia. His research centers on strategy and innovation in public policy and organization studies.

Robert Christensen

Brigham Young University

Robert Christensen is professor and George Romney Research Fellow in the Marriott School at Brigham Young University. His research focuses on prosocial and antisocial behaviors and attitudes in public and nonprofit organizations.

About the Series

The foundation of this series are cutting-edge contributions on emerging topics and definitive reviews of keystone topics in public and nonprofit administration, especially those that lack longer treatment in textbook or other formats. Among keystone topics of interest for scholars and practitioners of public and nonprofit administration, it covers public management, public budgeting and finance, nonprofit studies, and the interstitial space between the public and nonprofit sectors, along with theoretical and methodological contributions, including quantitative, qualitative and mixed-methods pieces.

The Public Management Research Association

The Public Management Research Association improves public governance by advancing research on public organizations, strengthening links among interdisciplinary scholars, and furthering professional and academic opportunities in public management.

Cambridge Elements ≡

Public and Nonprofit Administration

Printed in the United States
by Baker & Taylor Publisher Services